Adjudication in Construction Contracts — The Basics

CLIENTS — BUILDERS — ARCHITECTS — ENGINEERS — SURVEYORS

Adjudication in Construction Contracts — The Basics

A Guide to the Statutory Adjudication of Disputes
arising under Construction Contracts
and Related Professional Service Agreements

Tim Eaton

Published by the Author

Published by Tim Eaton at Wartha Manor, Lizard, Cornwall, TR12 7NR, UK

Phone & fax 01326 290084.

e-mail e@eaton.co.uk

British Library Cataloguing in Publication Data

A catalogue record for this book is available from the British Library

ISBN 0 9533464 0 4

Printed by

Antony Rowe Ltd., Chippenham, SN14 6LH UK

About the Author

Tim Eaton is a Chartered Architect with wide experience as designer and project manager for private and public works. He now specialises in dispute resolution working as an arbitrator, adjudicator, mediator and expert witness in construction, professional service, negligence and partnership disputes. He is a tutor on training courses for construction industry adjudicators.

Contents

Contents — Appendices

Preface

Disputes = (Time + Money + Effort) ^{STRESS}

During thirty five years experience as an architect in general practice, responsible for the design and project management of public and private sector building projects, large and small, and in my work in the resolution of other people's disputes, I have observed that most disputes arise from a failure to communicate requirements and intentions adequately or a failure to carry out instructions. Disputes are often escalated by the failure of the parties to negotiate effectively, and particularly by muddled and emotional thought.

Parties who have entered a contract to provide building design or construction services have done so in a state of mutual trust. Any problem which arises is normally dealt with by identification of issues, analysis and negotiation. When fault occurs, however trivial, disputants move from trust to caution. If the matter is not quickly resolved they might descend a scale through mistrust, entrenchment, embattlement to out-and-out enmity.

In 1965 when Honduras and El Salvador met each other in the preliminary rounds of the 1966 World Cup they played football against a very tense political background. That night, as the successful team returned home by road they were ambushed in the border hills and the resulting skirmish developed into a war between the armies of the two countries. You and I may differ about which football team we support but we are unlikely to come to blows. However, if I owe you money, you may pursue me through the courts.

When disputants find that they are unable to settle their differences they may resort to third parties for help. The international political mediators and the highest courts resolve the most complex disputes. In the construction industry, if the parties cannot settle matters amicably they have traditionally gone to litigation or arbitration to have a just settlement imposed upon them by a neutral judge or arbitrator. In over 90% of civil actions, the dispute is settled by mutual agreement before it comes to judgement. I believe that it is the escalation of cost in time, money and effort which causes the disputants to find settlement. To the inexperienced party these three factors are compounded by stress.

In 1998 the Government has provided disputants with the right of statutory adjudication to give rapid and relatively economical determination of disputes in construction contracts and related professional services agreements entered from 1st May 1998.

This guide is intended to introduce statutory adjudication in construction contracts to the inexperienced client and contractor, and to provide an outline working guide for the architect, engineer and surveyor. I will endeavour to place adjudication in the context of other methods of dispute resolution and to set out the adjudication process for all of those involved:- the disputant parties, other interested or affected parties and their professional advisers.

I have not included the text of The Act and Adjudication Rules but have provided a synopsis and commentary in a form which I hope will be easier for non-specialists to follow than the legal forms adopted in the text of such documents. I am an architect with a specialist interest and experience in dispute resolution. I must stress that I am not a lawyer, neither do I profess detailed knowledge of the law. If a reader needs advice on points of law and legal procedure he or she should consult an experienced lawyer.

Users of this guide, should be aware that I use the masculine pronoun throughout as a convention which implies no disrespect or favour to adjudicators, their clients, or their professional advisers.

T.E., Lizard. Cornwall, June 1998.

Glossary of Terms and Abbreviations

Act	The Housing Grants, Construction and Regeneration Act 1996 under which statutory adjudication is provided
Adjudication	Process of providing a decision which will determine a dispute
Adjudicator	The person who will decide in adjudication
ANB	Adjudicator Nominating Body
Arbitration	The process of action for determination of a dispute by an arbitrator under the provisions of The Arbitration Act 1996
CEDR	The Centre for Dispute Resolution
CIC MAP	The Construction Industry Council Model Adjudication Procedure
Contract	A binding agreement to provide a service for payment
Costs	The cost to the disputants of participation in a dispute resolution process
Party Costs	The costs incurred directly by the parties for advice and representation
Costs in the action	The costs accruing to the tribunal including fees, expenses and disbursements for advice
Decision	The decision reached by the adjudicator to determine a dispute
Disputant	A party in dispute with another
ICE	The Institution of Civil Engineers
JCT	The Joint Contracts Tribunal

Joint & Several liability	People jointly liable for a debt can be sued individually for the whole debt if one fails to pay
Litigation	The process of action for determination of a dispute by the courts of law
Notice of Adjudication	The notice of intention to refer a dispute to adjudication given by the referrer to another party to the dispute
ORSA	The Official Referees Solicitors Association
Party to a contract	A person or organisation, named as either employer or contractor
Party to a dispute	A party to the contract, being in dispute with another
Peremptory order	An order with an ultimatum which is to be effective if the order is not obeyed
Referral Notice	The notice setting out the dispute given by the referrer to the adjudicator
Referrer	The party who refers a dispute to adjudication
RIBA	The Royal Institute of British Architects
RICS	The Royal Institution of Chartered Surveyors
Scheme	The Scheme for Construction Contracts, default rules to apply where a contract does not comply with The Act
Tribunal	A person or group who will determine a dispute such as a judge, arbitrator or adjudicator

1. Introduction

When man became capable of reasoning with his fellows he began to negotiate. He soon found the need for a skilled third party to settle disputes. A trusted and respected elder would arbitrate. Finding a need for rules, the elders made laws and eventually, particularly in the western world, the legal profession developed to administer justice and to represent the disputants' interests. Our system of justice remains essentially adversarial. In some Pacific rim countries the social need to avoid loss of face has led to a preference for private settlement by mediated negotiation.

Construction can be a lengthy and often complex process. It is seldom in the interest of the parties for it to be delayed by wrangling. The construction industry has traditionally favoured arbitration in preference to litigation. A trusted expert hears evidence from both sides and the disputants accept his award. Having experienced the rapid resolution of disputes by adjudication in some standard engineering contracts and on large public civil engineering contracts, the construction industry asked Government to provide a statutory framework for adjudication.

The Housing Grants, Construction and Regeneration Act 1996, in Part II, Construction — which I call The Act — provides the right to refer a dispute for adjudication. The Act contains adjudication rules which must be included in a contract, perhaps with other procedures, such as those published in JCT standard forms, or under a contract as a separate scheme of rules. If a contract fails to make this provision, The Scheme for Construction Contracts — which I call The Scheme — applies by default.

The party who receives a Notice of Adjudication may be unaware that it was coming and may be ambushed at an inconvenient time. It is important that contractors, clients and their professional advisors know what to do on receipt of a Notice of Adjudication. Prompt and appropriate reactions are essential. The adjudicator's decision will be based on a strict analysis of the contract documents, variations and instructions, not on guts and sympathy.

2. Dispute Resolution in Construction Contracts

2.1 Box 1 Must a Dispute be Resolved?

One	"It's only the 1st of April, I don't need to pay yet."	A statement of fact
Two	"No it is not. It is the 1st of May."	A difference
One	"Does it matter?"	One does not care
Two	"Yes!"	A dispute to be resolved
One	"Can we negotiate?"	One is conciliatory
Two	"NO!"	A neutral third party is needed to help
Three	"Can I mediate between you?"	A helper at hand
One	"Yes please."	Settlement might be achieved by mutual agreement
Two	"Oh, no, I want a third party to finally determine this matter."	SOS
Four	"I am an Adjudicator / Arbitrator / Judge. I will determine the matter and impose my decision on you both."	
One	"What if I do not accept your decision?"	
Four	"Two can then ask for a Court Order to enforce it."	
One	"What if I ignore the Order?"	
Four	"You may be sent to prison for contempt of court!"	

Moral:- Keep talking to each other and negotiate resolution amicably.

2.2 Negotiation

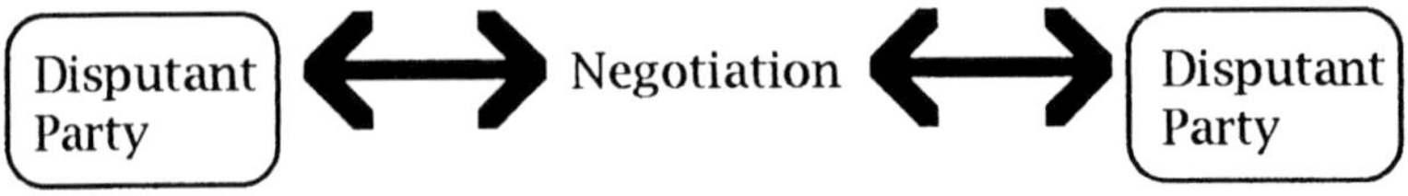

We all negotiate throughout our lives, whether for pocket money, in domestic differences, or at work. In an ideal world we would all be able to negotiate quickly and effectively and never fall out with each other. Sadly this is not an ideal world.

Successful negotiation depends on principled argument and on avoiding causing loss of face. A bitter haggle based on grudging retreat by stages from a series of posed fixed positions is not good negotiation; it is a western misconception that such haggling is how negotiations are conducted in the souk.

The carpet merchant makes deals with his customers through a ritual process in which both sides make allowances to the other until they reach an amicable settlement which both find reasonable. They will have sat in the shop, drinking tea, discussing football, and showing each other pictures of their children. They start as strangers and finish with mutual respect and trust. If the customer was to accept the first price offered by the merchant, the merchant would suffer a guilty conscience at having cheated the customer; if either behaves unreasonably, the process fails.

Even in minor purchases in an Eastern market, exchanges are traded:-

"You are my first customer today — yesterday I had no-one. I will make a good price for you. I will make you very happy."

"To be happy I would need two for your price."

A few minutes later the merchant is honoured by his first sale of the day, to this same customer. He has sold one widget for half the price of two; life is looking up.

In commercial negotiation it is essential that the parties each carry authority to settle. Valuation disputes where the surveyors do not have discretion to move beyond an imposed limit are sooner resolved by a meeting of their bosses. I believe that most disputes could be settled by two well briefed managing directors after a good lunch.

2.3 ADR — Mediation

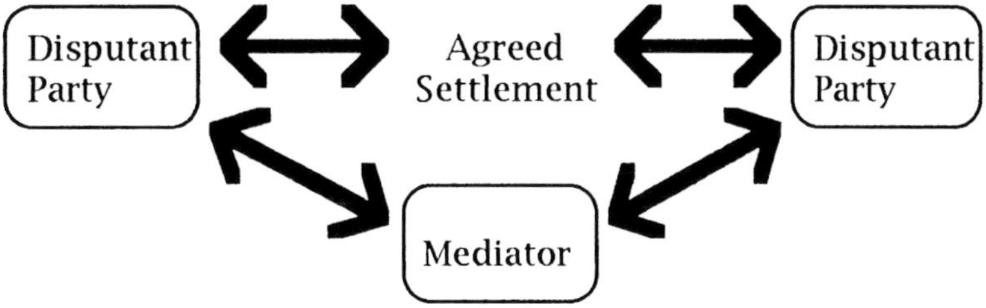

ADR, or Alternative Dispute Resolution, is a ragbag term which came to Britain from America in the 1980s. It covered the other methods of dispute resolution which were then the alternatives to the statutory processes of litigation and arbitration and developed in reaction to the long waiting lists in the courts. Although it embraces processes which are only voluntarily binding, such as expert determination, and even rent-a-judge, the core of ADR is mediation and conciliation. These two terms are often transposed in their definitions. In the one, the third party will only pass messages, in the other he is more pro-active, and mediation is emerging as the more generally used term. A trusted neutral third party, trained as a mediator, discusses the issues with the parties together and independently. The mediator builds trust with the parties. The mediator will hold the confidential disclosures of each party —the hidden agenda which may not be disclosed to the other disputant. He will help each party to understand the other party's argument and he will discuss each party's options, particularly the best and worst options. The mediator is skilled in allowing the party to discharge emotional stress on the way to a reasoned solution. The outcome of a commercial dispute which could put a sub-contractor into liquidation might be resolved by a company merger, to the long term benefit of both companies. This would not emerge as an option in the statutory processes.

2.4 Litigation

The dispute follows the normal legal processes through the courts. The disputants take on the roles of plaintiff and defendant and have their case argued on their behalf by lawyers before a judge. Experts are called by each side to report and give evidence of their independent opinion to the court. It may be two or more years after entering legal proceedings before judgement is obtained in the court of first instance. If the unsuccessful party wishes to take the matter to a higher court he will appeal in the High Court. He may even take it beyond, to the House of Lords and to Europe. At each stage the costs of the successful litigant may be ordered to be paid by the unsuccessful adversary and the costs can easily exceed the value of the claim. The parties, becoming entrenched, regard the process as a bitter battle about a point of principle. The pragmatism of the loss adjuster or the skilled negotiator is often set aside so that the litigation process becomes a bitter crusade.

Although litigation is the only sure way to settle a dispute which depends on interpretation of the law, it is expensive, time consuming and stressful for the disputants. Technical issues are better resolved by technical experts.

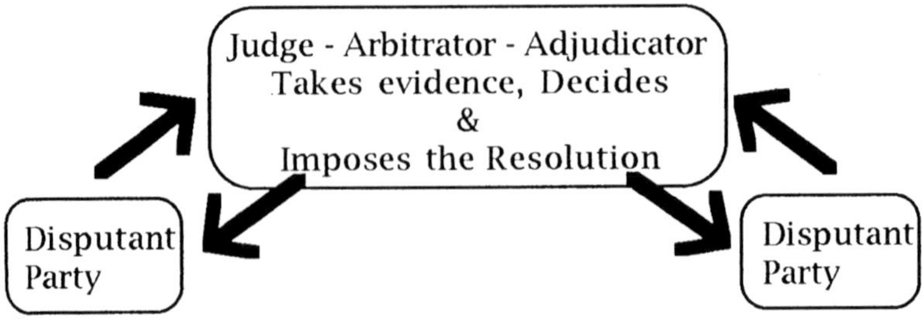

2.5 Arbitration

Arbitration has developed from the traditional trade practice of informal arbitration, depending on the good faith of the claimant and the respondent to be bound by the award of a mutually trusted expert. The process now largely mimics the process of litigation, the difference being that the expert arbitrator will understand the technicalities of the dispute which in litigation might have to be explained to the lawyers who would then seek to explain it in non-technical terms to the judges. It takes place in private. Pleadings usually follow the sequence of legal proceedings with Points of Claim, Defence and Counterclaim, Defence to the Counterclaim, and so on. Arbitration in Britain is now subject to The Arbitration Act 1996 which does go some way towards providing a more efficient and user-friendly process than the previous Acts. It remains a relatively lengthy and expensive process, although the parties have opportunities to make the process quicker and more cost effective. The arbitrator has the opportunity to manage the process and to cap the budget for recoverable costs if he feels that one party may spend excessively on obtaining expert reports and legal advice and representation. Arbitration has the great advantage that, unless the arbitrator has made some procedural error, the High Court will uphold an arbitrator's award without any discretion to look into the pleadings. There is no appeal available.

Most construction and professional service agreements contain an arbitration clause which says that disputes under the contract will be settled by arbitration. This has the effect of ensuring that the defendant in a case which is first brought in litigation can ask the court to set the case aside to allow arbitration to take precedence. Construction arbitrators are usually architects, engineers or surveyors depending whether the dispute is about technical matters or valuation.

Small claims courts often hear cases with the judge sitting as an arbitrator rather than as a judge so that the disputants can present their cases without the more strict procedural rules of court practice. The judge can be satisfied that an unrepresented party has a full and fair opportunity to express his case clearly in his own terms. It has the side effect of removing the opportunity of appeal.

2.6 Adjudication

Time is usually of the essence in construction projects and the cost of work delayed while arguments are held is not usually in the interest of the parties, particularly if plant or labour is idle. Construction is a pragmatic process and it is usually in the interest of the parties that problems are settled quickly so that the project can proceed without delay. If contentious argument is to continue at a later date, it can then be settled by an allocation of cost after the works are complete.

Sir Michael Latham, in *Constructing the Team* advocated adjudication or mediation in alternative dispute resolution (ADR) to save time and money in construction disputes. Although ADR is slowly gaining ground, the construction industry took Latham's recommendations to Parliament and demanded legislation to make rapid adjudication available throughout the industry, both in contracting and in the supporting professional services of design and advice.

Adjudication has come to be the term for a quick determination of matters in dispute by a neutral third party without the thorough processes of litigation or arbitration. In many cases this will be sufficient and the parties will accept the adjudicator's decision as binding. The following quotation from clause 1.1 of the ICE Adjudication Procedure is appropriate to all adjudication:-

"The object of adjudication under this procedure is to reach a fair, rapid and inexpensive determination of a dispute arising under the contract and this procedure shall be interpreted accordingly."

However, since speed may mean that it is not conducted under such rigorous procedures, it cannot be enforceable as a finally binding determination of the dispute unless the parties so agree; it may only act as a working decision until or unless it is tested more thoroughly in arbitration or litigation.

2.6.1 Statutory Adjudication — The Act

The Housing Grants, Construction and Regeneration Act 1996, at Part II, Construction, which is effective for construction contracts entered from 1 May 1998 onwards, introduced a statutory right for any party to a construction contract or to a related professional services agreement to refer most disputes unilaterally to an adjudicator for a decision within 28 days. The adjudicator will normally be an architect, an engineer or a surveyor, depending on the matters in dispute.

The Act defines construction operations and contracts very widely and sets a few basic rules which should be provided either in, or under a contract. They are, essentially:-

- the right to refer a dispute at any time,
- to an adjudicator appointed within 7 days,
- who will act impartially,
- to ascertain the facts and the law,
- and give a decision within a further 28 days,
- which will be immediately binding,
- or until found otherwise in arbitration or litigation;
- the Adjudicator not being liable for acts or omissions, unless in bad faith.

Note:- The Act is outlined at Appendix A and it has been modified by an Exclusion Order which is outlined at Appendix B.

2.6.2 Schemes of Rules for Adjudication

Contracts should include at least the provisions of s.108 (1) - (4) of The Act. These will either be included as clauses in the body of the contract, or by reference to a subsidiary scheme of rules which will operate under the contract. Failure to include such provision will, by default, automatically bring The Scheme for Construction Contracts into force. This will particularly be so when the agreement is made by an exchange of letters or evidenced or recorded in some other informal way.

Note:- The Scheme for Construction Contracts is outlined at Appendix C.

Standard forms, such as The Joint Contracts Tribunal (JCT) contracts, include standard schemes, such as the JCT Rules for Adjudication. They also include standard forms of agreement for the adjudicator's services. JCT philosophy is that there should not be complex rules. The Adjudicator should be enabled to manage the process to produce a sound decision quickly and economically.

Note:- JCT Rules for Adjudication are outlined at Appendix D.

The Institution of Civil Engineers (ICE) publishes standard forms of contract which refer to the ICE Adjudication Procedure. This procedure can be made suitable for any contract with minor amendments.

Note:- ICE Adjudication Procedure is outlined at Appendix E.

The Construction Industry Council represents the contractors' organisations and the construction professional institutions and was keen that Government should adopt its model as the Government Scheme. To the dismay of many observers Government thought otherwise and produced a different Scheme. The Construction Industry Council Model Adjudication Procedure (CIC MAP) rules are well set out and are suitable for construction contracts and professional services agreements alike. Professional Institutions such as the RIBA intend to introduce CIC MAP as the rules for their standard forms for professional appointments.

Note:- CIC MAP is outlined at Appendix F.

Various other organisations also publish rules for adjudication suitable for inclusion in construction contracts. These include The Centre for Dispute Resolution, (CEDR) and The Official Referees Solicitors Association (ORSA).

CEDR is the principal organisation concerned with alternative dispute resolution, ADR. Its interests cover other forms of dispute resolution than litigation and arbitration, principally mediation. CEDR members include most of the larger firms of solicitors, many barristers and some judges, with a smaller number of non-legal professional people. CEDR has published its own Rules for Adjudication and standard adjudication clauses for contracts. It also acts as an adjudicator appointing body independently of the professional institutions and provides adjudication services. CEDR Rules have a feature not found in most of the other schemes: the decision is deemed finally binding unless a party gives a notice of dissatisfaction within 60 days of the decision.

Note:- CEDR Rules for Adjudication are outlined at Appendix G.

ORSA serves solicitors who specialise in construction disputes in the Official Referees' courts and in arbitration. ORSA Adjudication Rules are drafted by lawyers for lawyers and are tied to ORSA as an administrating body and an adjudicator nominating body. They give the adjudicator wide discretion to conduct the adjudication and to widen its scope as he thinks fit, but they back up that liberality with provision for the Chairman of ORSA to take action if a party complains to ORSA about the conduct of the adjudicator.

Note:- ORSA Adjudication Rules are outlined at Appendix H.

3. Contracts falling under The Act

3.1 Box 2 Does The Act Apply?

Does The Act apply to the work in the contract?

Check the text of The Act (see Appendix A for an outline):-

S.104 Is the work Construction, Design or Advice...?

If No, Stop.
If Yes, See next.

S.105 ...for Construction Operations as described & not excluded...?

Check also in Exclusion Orders (see Appendix B for an outline.)
If No, Stop.
If Yes, See next.

S.106 ...principally to the Dwelling of a Party ...in a house or flat as defined...?

If Yes, Stop.
If No, See next.

S.107 ...by an agreement written,

...evidenced in writing,

...or somehow recorded

If No, Stop.
If Yes, Statutory Adjudication is available under S.108.

See Box 3 — The Adjudication Rules

3.2 Contracts falling under The Act — Summary

Note:- For an outline of the works which are covered by The Act for the purposes of statutory adjudication see Appendix A.

Sections 104 to 107, which define construction contracts for the purpose of The Act, are relevant to adjudication, with S.115 — Service of Notice, and S.116 — Reckoning Time and Dates.

S.104 contains a wide description of what is considered to be a construction contract under The Act. There is no minimum size, value or duration. All stages in the procurement and maintenance of buildings are effectively included, from advice, design, and surveying in relation to construction operations to the carrying out, or arranging for, or providing labour for construction operations. It is clear that any service related to construction operations will be potentially included. Only work under a contract of employment is specifically excluded.

S.105 (1) defines construction operations and also employs very wide terms. It starts with a range, from construction and maintenance, to demolition of buildings or structures and civil engineering works. It goes on to include mechanical, electrical and services engineering installations, cleaning in connection with all these activities, and integral or preparatory operations such as ground works through scaffolding to landscaping, and painting and decorating.

S.105 (2) contains exclusions, mainly related to mineral extraction, plant, machinery and steelwork for some manufacturing industries. The manufacture of components and equipment for supply only is excluded but not if it is to be supplied and installed. Artistic works are excluded.

S.106 provides a narrow definition of exclusion of dwellings for a party to the contract. Most housing work will not be excluded.

S.107 defines the contract or agreement in wide terms, from written contracts to agreements evidenced in writing, not written but referring to written terms, and those recorded by any means.

An answering machine message asking for the gutters to be painted would be the basis a construction contract and just as valid as a very detailed contract for a billion pound office development with its head in the clouds.

As a result of political lobbying, The Construction Contracts (England and Wales) Exclusion Order 1998 — and the Scottish equivalent — has introduced more categories of building which are excluded from the operation of The Act.

Note:- The Exclusion Orders are outlined at Appendix B.

4. Providing for Adjudication in the Contract

If the contract is for construction works or related professional services of design or advice as set out in The Act at S.104 to S.107 — and not excluded by the Exclusion Orders — adjudication is provided in S.108 as a statutory right which can not be extinguished.

4.1 Box 3 Adjudication Rules in or under the Contract?

Is Statutory Adjudication provided for in the Contract?

If Not, The Government Scheme for Construction Contracts applies by default.

Is there an Adjudication Clause in the Contract?

If Not, The Scheme for Construction Contracts applies. Stop.

If Yes, check the clause.

Does the Adjudication Clause provide that

any disputes or differences arising under the Contract

will be dealt with by Adjudication?

If Not, The Scheme for Construction Contracts applies. Stop.
If Yes, check the clause.

Does the Clause include rules which comply with The Act

S.108 (1) to (4)?

If Yes, e.g. JCT80 cl.41A, Adjudication proceeds under the Clause. Stop.
If Not, Continue checking the Clause

Does the Clause refer to a free-standing Adjudication Procedure?

If Not, The Scheme for Construction Contracts will apply. Stop.
If Yes, e.g. CICMAP, ICE, CEDR, ORSA, Check the Procedure referred to.

Does the Procedure comply with The Act S.108 (1) to (4)?

If No, The Scheme for Construction Contracts will apply. Stop.

If Yes, The Procedure referred to will apply.

The choice to be made when the contract terms are being drafted relates only to the rules under which the adjudication is to be conducted, and whether an adjudicator, or an adjudicator nominating body, is to be chosen in advance (see Section 5.1 Choosing an Adjudicator).

The Act provides a few over-riding rules in S.108 (1) to (4) which apply to all contracts.

They may be covered either:-

a) by writing rules, including S.108 (1) - (4), into the contract directly, or

b) by referring in the contract to a set of compliant rules which will apply under the contract.

Failure to include compliant rules by one of the above alternative means will result in the Government's Scheme applying by default.

Any other rules may be added, provided that they do not conflict with The Act.

Informal agreements such as those caught under the provisions of s.107 of The Act — contracts evidenced in writing or recorded by other means — will almost always include no adjudication procedure and default to The Scheme.

4.2 Adjudication Rules written into the Contract

Any organisation which decides to draft its own terms of agreement may write in an adjudication procedure. As the barest minimum S.108 (1) to (4) could be reproduced as terms of the contract. However, rather than doing this it would probably be better to ignore them so that The Scheme would apply. They are minimal and the construction industry has provided more detailed rules which are suitable for adoption.

Some standard forms of contract published by various bodies include clauses to provide the rules which those bodies favour. The Joint Contract Tribunal forms of contract include the JCT Adjudication Clause and the JCT Adjudication Agreement. These are drafted specifically to relate to the particular form of contract, and in JCT contracts, with the substantial baggage of case law which follows JCT contracts, it would be unwise to take out such clauses.

In most cases, if the contract is not to be left void of adjudication provision, the easier way to incorporate rules is to attach a ready-made scheme to apply under the contract. The adjudication clause in the contract should say that any difference or dispute arising under the contract must be referred for adjudication under a designated scheme of rules.

4.3 Adjudication Rules to operate under the Contract

Most of the schemes of adjudication rules which have been provided by the industry and construction lawyers' organisations, are designed to be referred to in the contract, and to stand separately under the contract. Any such scheme must comply with The Act as otherwise it would fail and The Scheme would apply by default.

Other than JCT, which is written in the contract, the scheme most widely adopted by construction industry professionals is likely to be the Construction Industry Council's Model Adjudication Procedure (CICMAP). It is designed to be used both for construction works or for professional services agreements and provides a good self-contained scheme to suit most purposes.

Similarly, standard engineering contracts published by ICE are supported by ICE Adjudication Procedures.

There are two schemes which are drafted by lawyer-led organisations. The ORSA Rules and CEDR Rules are both drafted to reflect construction litigation lawyers' views rather than builders' and construction professionals' experience-based approach. They are facilitative of a quick decision without legal intervention.

CEDR provides two alternative model clauses for insertion in the contract, alternative B being a concise form also suitable for any other scheme of rules.

ORSA suggests incorporation of adjudication by suitable wording along the following lines:-

"Any dispute arising under this agreement shall in the first instance be referred to adjudication in accordance with the ORSA Adjudication Rules."

In place of the reference to ORSA Adjudication Rules, any other compliant rules could be referred to: The Scheme for Construction Contracts, CICMAP, CEDR, ICE etc..

The various schemes of rules are outlined above — see *2.6.2 Schemes of Rules for Adjudication*; commentaries are provided in the Appendices.

5. Preparation for Adjudication

5.1 Box 4 Choosing an Adjudicator

An Adjudicator should be appointed within 7 days of the notice of intention to refer a dispute for adjudication
— The Notice of Adjudication

Is an Adjudicator named in the Contract?

If Yes,	Ask if he is available. He should reply within 2 days. If he is, refer the dispute to him within 7 days of the Notice.
If Not,	See next.

Can the Parties agree an adjudicator within 2 days of the Notice?

If Yes,	Ask if he is available. He should reply within 2 days. If he is, refer the dispute to him within 7 days of the Notice.
If Not,	See next.

Is an Adjudicator Nominating Body named in the Contract?

If Yes,	Ask the Body to nominate an adjudicator within 5 days.
Then	Ask him if he is available. He should reply within 2 days. If he is, refer the dispute to him within 7 days of the Notice, or as soon as possible.
If Not,	See next.

Can the Parties agree a Nominating Body within 2 days.

If Yes,	Proceed as above, ask for a Nomination, appoint etc..
If Not,	The Referrer chooses a Nominating Body and asks for a name as above.

Once the Adjudicator is named, agreed, or nominated,

the Referrer appoints him.

The other party cannot reject him.

Note that some bodies appoint rather than nominate the Adjudicator.

The above procedure will re-cycle until an Adjudicator accepts.

5.2 Choosing an Adjudicator

An adjudicator must be what the law calls "a natural person", not an organisation. An adjudicator may be chosen by the parties to a contract in several ways. He may be:-

- chosen by the employer and named in the contract during drafting;
- chosen by the parties and name inserted when the contract is entered;
- chosen by the parties when a dispute arises;
- selected by an Adjudicator Nominating Body which itself may be named in the contract, chosen by the employer, or by the parties.

There are advantages and disadvantages to each method. It is important to bear in mind that The Act requires a procedure which has the objective of securing an appointment within 7 days of the Notice of Adjudication.

The disadvantage of choosing an adjudicator before a dispute arises is that he may not be the most suitable person for the particular dispute when it does arise. An architect chosen in advance may then be called to resolve an engineering or surveying dispute and may decide that he cannot accept the referral. Alternatively he may decide to act but to call in advice from an engineer or surveyor at extra cost to the disputants.

5.2.1 Naming in the Contract

If an adjudicator is named in the contract he will be called if and when a dispute arises. He should be asked to confirm that he is willing to be named and to confirm that he will keep the parties informed about his availability so that they do not call him just as he goes on holiday. This can be done at minimal cost. If the parties decide to keep him informed about the contract, by copies of the monthly progress meeting minutes for example, he will require to be paid a retainer.

If the employer chooses the adjudicator and inserts his name while drafting the contract for tender, the adjudicator may be seen by the contractor as potentially biased — the employer's favourite adjudicator.

A more equitable way of naming the adjudicator in the contract is for the parties to agree a name after they have agreed the contract. A mutually acceptable name is then inserted.

It will generally be better to name an architect or engineer, depending on the type of construction, as most disputes are about the works and the surveyor's role is to deal with the measurement and valuation of quantum following a decision of an architect or engineer.

5.2.2 Naming an Adjudicator Nominating Body in the Contract

Adjudicator Nominating Bodies are those which undertake to maintain a list of adjudicators who may be nominated by the Body for a particular dispute when it arises.

Referral to a Nominating Body removes any conflict of trust between the parties who might otherwise argue about who to appoint. That Body will then be prepared to nominate an adjudicator at very short notice to comply with the rules for the particular dispute.

If a professional institution is named in the contract it will generally be the institution of the profession whose member is in overall charge of the contract. Institutions such as the RIBA, ICE, RICS maintain multi-disciplinary lists of people who are qualified to an acceptable standard, regularly vetted, and who are willing to be nominated:-

Royal Institute of British Architects	RIBA	mainly architect-adjudicators
Institution of Civil Engineers	ICE	mainly engineer-adjudicators
Royal Institution of Chartered Surveyors	RICS	mainly surveyor-adjudicators
Chartered Institute of Arbitrators	CIArb	all the above and lawyers
Centre for Dispute Resolution	CEDR	mainly lawyers, some others.

The Government maintains a list of Adjudicator Nominating Bodies but defines them only as those who hold themselves out as such. This last provision has inherent dangers. There is no governmental system of vetting the adjudicator nominating bodies, or the people who they nominate. In the interest of consumer protection the Construction Industry Council is co-ordinating the nominating function of suitable bodies to ensure that their nominated adjudicators are trained and their performance monitored to a common standard.

It would be prudent to go only to a professional institution or a reputable body like CEDR which is on the CIC list.

5.2.3 Choosing an Adjudicator when the need arises

If the parties can agree on a person to act as adjudicator, choosing him after the dispute has arisen does have the advantage that he will be seen by the parties as suitable. This might be the ideal situation; however once parties are involved in conflict they often find it difficult to agree who should determine it for them and a provision for an institution to choose should always be included.

5.2.4 Finding an Adjudicator when needed.

If there is no named adjudicator, no named body and the parties cannot agree on a name, under most of the rules, the referrer can then go unilaterally to any Adjudicator Nominating Body to ask for a nomination.

5.3 The Notice of Adjudication

5.3.1 The Referrer's Notice

The Act provides that a party has the right at any time to refer a dispute for adjudication by giving notice of his intention to do so. The Scheme calls this notice the Notice of Adjudication. Other rules may vary the name of the notice but its function is the same.

The Act does not say who the Notice is to be given to. In a multi-party contract it may suffice to give it only to the other disputant. The Scheme clearly states that it should be given to every other party to the contract and this should be the normal procedure at the outset even though the subsequent stages may be between the disputant parties.

The Scheme rules that the notice of adjudication shall set out briefly:-

a) the nature and a brief description of the dispute and of the parties involved,

b) details of where and when the dispute has arisen,

c) the nature of the redress which is sought,

d) the names and addresses of the parties to the contract (including, where appropriate, the addresses which the parties have specified for the giving of notices).

Giving the notice starts the clock for the seven days during which the adjudicator should be appointed.

The Act counts all days except Christmas Day, Good Friday and Bank Holidays — weekend days are included in the seven days.

A major criticism of The Act is that the unilateral right to start the process with a notice also gives the wily party an opportunity to ambush the other disputant at an inconvenient time. Adjudicator Nominating Bodies under The Scheme must nominate an adjudicator within five days and the adjudicator must confirm acceptance, or decline within two days. It should be only if an adjudicator declines to act that the process will go beyond the overall seven days of The Act.

5.3.2 The Referrer's Brief Statement

Within seven days of the Notice of Adjudication the matter is referred to an adjudicator. The Scheme provides that this is done by sending him a written Referral Notice, accompanied by copies of, or relevant extracts from the construction contract and such other documents as the referring party intends to rely on. This bundle is sent at the same time to every other party to the dispute.

It is desirable that the Referral Notice should also be accompanied by a brief statement which amplifies the particulars given in the Notice of Adjudication. Some bodies limit the length of such a statement. It should not be more than about five A4 sides. It should give sufficient of the referrer's case argument to allow the other disputants to prepare their answering argument. Its other function is to give the adjudicator sufficient knowledge of the dispute to make directions for procedure.

5.3.3 Other Parties

It is important to distinguish between the other parties. In a multi-party contract all parties must know what is happening so that they can protect their own interests. The decision of the adjudicator may affect them adversely. If they are not parties to the dispute they might not be involved in the proceedings in which case they effectively become interested third parties. The Scheme distinguishes between *parties to the contract* and *parties to the dispute.*

5.4 Appointment of the Adjudicator

5.4.1 Adjudicators' Terms of Appointment

For his contract with the disputants it may be sufficient that he is instructed. The law provides a right to reasonable fees and expenses. The Scheme provides him with entitlement to such reasonable amount as he may determine by way of fees and expenses reasonably incurred by him. It also makes the parties jointly and severally responsible for paying him. This means that if one party defaults on payment, the others must make up the deficit. On being invited to adjudicate the adjudicator will wish to make clear his terms, particularly for payment of his charges and expenses, and for things such as time set aside which may be wasted if arrangements are not followed.

It is conventional for professionals acting in contentious work to require the security of funds in hand for their charges — payment up front. This is normally done by the parties' making payments on account which the adjudicator will keep in his client account and only draw down when he has earned them.

The parties may agree to pay half each of any fees on account. This avoids any effect that failure of one party to keep the adjudicator in funds may have on his partiality. Alternatively, the referrer may decide to fund the referral, subject to the adjudicator finally allocating cost between the disputants when he has made his decision.

Whether or not he has secured funds from the parties the adjudicator will almost certainly want an arrangement in his terms which provides payment in full before he releases his decision. Some rules may allow for this, for example by allowing the adjudicator to give seven days' notice before providing the decision. The Scheme only requires him to give a copy to the disputants as soon as possible after he has reached his decision.

The decision will not alter the liability of the parties to third parties through the contract — the parties should not be able to off-load liability onto the adjudicator. Some rules provide indemnity for the adjudicator against the action of third parties who might be adversely affected by his decision. Adjudicators may require specific indemnity in their terms of appointment.

5.4.2 Timetable for the Appointment

All adjudication procedures are bound by the provision of The Act that they should have the objective of making it possible to appoint the adjudicator within 7 days of the Notice of Adjudication. The timetable for the appointment is set out in the various schemes of rules. These can be quite complex, with differing periods for nominating an adjudicator in the second round which follows if an an adjudicator declines to act. What they have in common is the provision of The Act that it should be possible to complete the appointment within seven days of the Notice of Adjudication. The process must be completed whatever the prior commitments of the parties and this places a burden on the non-referring party.

If an adjudicator declines an appointment, or an Adjudicator Nominating Body fails to nominate within the timescale, this does not halt the process. The procedure re-cycles until an effective appointment has been made, and it is the provision that each stage is only a few days long, for agreeing a name, or agreeing a Nominating Body, obtaining a nomination and obtaining the adjudicator's acceptance, with defaults to allow the referrer to maintain progress and to seize the initiative unilaterally if the other party is not co-operative.

6. The Referrers' Actions in the Adjudication

6.1 Box 5 What must the Referrer do?

Day 1

The Referrer serves a Notice of Adjudication stating intent to refer.
The Referrer refers the dispute to the Adjudicator named in the contract.
If no Adjudicator is named in the contract,
the Referrer & the Other Party agree an Adjudicator.

Day 3 If not agreed:-

the Referrer asks the Adjudicator Nominating Body (ANB) named in the contract to nominate.
If no ANB is named, the Referrer & the Other Party agree an ANB.

Day 5 If not agreed:-

the Referrer unilaterally selects an ANB
and requests a nomination.

Most ANBs nominate. The Referrer obtains acceptance and appoints.
Note that some bodies appoint, subject to the Adjudicator's accepting.

Day 7 or soon after = Referral Day or R Day

By now the Adjudicator should be appointed.
Sending the Referral Notice to the Adjudicator starts the clock.

Note that in some rules R Day is the date of the Referral Notice;
in others, it is when the Adjudicator receives the Referral Notice;
or the date the Adjudicator acknowledges the Referral Notice.

The Referrer refers the dispute to the Adjudicator with:-
The Notice of Adjudication,
Details of the Parties,
Copy of the Contract,
Brief details of the issues,
Detail of the remedy being sought,
& copies everything to the Other Party.

D Day the Decision is due within 28 days of R Day, unless extended.

6.2 The Notice of Adjudication

The Notice of Adjudication is the document which starts the adjudication proceedings by the referring party's giving notice to the other parties to the contract that he intends to refer a dispute to adjudication.

The Notice starts the clock on any procedure for the appointment of an adjudicator which may apply under rules embodied in the contract. The Act requires that there should be a procedure which should result in appointment within 7 days of the Notice of Adjudication.

A party who receives the notice may have been unaware that it was coming and may even be ambushed as he prepares to go on holiday. It is important that contractors, clients and their professional advisors know what to do on receipt of a Notice of Adjudication. If the adjudicator has not been named in the contract at the outset, most procedures require agreement on a name within 2 days, failing which an Adjudicator Nominating Body will be asked for a name. They must provide a name quickly so that the adjudicator is able to confirm his availability and for the Referral Notice to be sent within 7 days of the Notice of Adjudication.

The Scheme requires the following set out briefly:-

(a) the nature & brief description of dispute and parties involved,

(b) details where & when it has arisen,

(c) redress which is sought,

(d) names and addresses of Parties to the Contract.

Other rules may differ but will be broadly similar.

6.3 Box 6 Typical Notice of Adjudication

A B Contracting Ltd. letterhead

addressed to C D Exploitation Ltd. Dated

By fax and 1st Class Post

Dear Sirs,

<u>Notice of Adjudication in respect of Brickwork</u>

This letter is to give you notice of our intention to refer our difference about the quality of, and payment for brickwork to an adjudicator under the provision of The Housing Grants, Construction and Regeneration Act 1996...

{A.1 if the contract provides for adjudication}

... and of the contract and of the...

{whichever procedural rules are in the contract; JCT, CIC, ICE, etc.}

... adjudication procedure.

{A.2 if the contract makes no provision for adjudication}

... and of The Scheme for Construction Contracts.

1 The particulars are as follows:-

1.1 We built brickwork as specified. We contend that the Contract Administrator's decision to value it as "shoddy" rather than "fair-faced" is not acceptable.

1.2 When the walls were built and rejected by the Clerk of Works, he wanted it rebuilt but the Architect/ Contract Administrator decided to let it stand. The Quantity Surveyor told us that the Architect had instructed him to value the wall as "shoddy brickwork" where the Specification calls for "fair-faced brickwork". If we are not going to be properly paid we would rather rebuild the wall but now the Architect says it is too late for that.

1.3 We consider that we are entitled to payment for fair-faced brickwork, or alternatively, to be permitted to rebuild the wall to the Clerk of Works's satisfaction and be allowed extra time for this.

1.4 The names and addresses of the parties in the contract are as given at the head of this Notice.

2 You will be aware that an adjudicator should be appointed within 7 days of this Notice.

{C. Selection of the Adjudicator—Alternatives are given}

{C.1 If an adjudicator is named in the contract}

Ms. A. J-K Fairlie being named in the contract as the adjudicator, we are copying this Notice to her today.

{C.2 If there is no adjudicator named but an ANB is named}

There being no adjudicator named in the contract we propose to appoint Ms. A. Judy-Kate Fairlie RIBA, The Scales, Willponder, UP2 ME2. Please confirm your agreement within 2 days failing which we shall ask for a Nomination by the President of the RIBA as the Adjudicator Nominating Body named in the contract.

OR

{C.3 If there is neither adjudicator nor an ANB named in the contract}

There being neither adjudicator nor Adjudicator Nominating Body named in the contract we propose to appoint Ms. A. Judy-Kate Fairlie RIBA, The Scales, Willponder, UP2 ME2. Please confirm your agreement within 2 days, or confirm your agreement to the RIBA as the Adjudicator Nominating Body, failing which we will unilaterally request nomination by an Adjudicator Nominating Body of our choice.

We look forward to hearing from you within two days in response to the above proposals, failing which we will proceed to obtain the nomination of an adjudicator within seven days of today.

As ever, we are willing to negotiate a reasonable settlement, rather than resort to adjudication. Perhaps we could discuss it over a sandwich at the Old Morgue and Skelett.

Yours faithfully,

6.4 The Referral Notice

Once the adjudicator is agreed by the parties, or nominated by an Adjudicator Nominating Body, the matter is referred to him for adjudication. The adjudicator's decision is normally required as soon as possible and within 28 days. The count of 28 days starts with the referral and it is important to be aware that different schemes of rules may define that date differently.

The Scheme defines it as the date of the referral notice; time in the post between the referrer and the adjudicator is lost and it might be appropriate for the parties to agree to send all communications by fax as well as post in order to avoid postal delays.

JCT, ICE and CICMAP use the date of the adjudicator's receiving the notice. CEDR uses either the date of CEDR's appointment of the Adjudicator, or, if he has been named in the contract, the date of his confirmation of acceptance. ORSA uses the date of his confirmation of acceptance.

It is essential that the particular rule is understood. In the event of any uncertainty it is safer to assume that the earliest, the date of the Notice, is the start date.

The referrer sends the Referral Notice to the adjudicator with sufficient information to enable him to give directions for the conduct of the adjudication. He will normally require:-

- the Notice of Adjudication with any attachments,
- the contract or agreement under which the dispute has arisen,
- a brief statement and such other documents as the referrer intends to rely on.

At the same time, the referrer sends copies of all of the above to the other parties to the dispute.

6.5 Box 7 Typical Referral Notice

AB Contracting Ltd. letterhead

addressed to Ms. A Judy-Kate Fairlie, RIBA

copied to C D Exploitation Ltd.

By fax and by 1st Class Post

Dear Ms. Fairlie,

Referral Notice for Adjudication in respect of Brickwork

As you are aware, you have been nominated by the RIBA to act as Adjudicator in our dispute with CD Exploitation Ltd..

Thank you for accepting the nomination so promptly. We agree to your terms as set out in your letter dated >>>.

This letter is to give notice of our referral of the matter to you for adjudication in accordance with the contract and The Housing Grants, Construction and Regeneration Act 96 under the {insert reference to the rules} Adjudication Procedure, and to appoint you.

We attach the following:-

The Notice of Adjudication dated >>>,

The Contract dated >>> between us and CDE,

Our Statement of Case,

Photocopies of the specification for brickwork,

Drawings nos. >>> showing the wall in dispute,

Our site diary for >>>, showing the entry recording the Clerk of Works's comments highlighted in yellow,

Architect's Instruction no. >>>,

Interim Certificate no. >>> with a valuation sheet detailing the QS's calculations for valuation,

We request you to visit the site to inspect the wall.

We await your directions.

Yours sincerely

6.6 The Referrer's Statement

The referrer's case is made in a statement which is supported by evidence in the form of documents, and by reference to any witnesses, and to any evidence to be seen on site.

The adjudication is to take place within a limited timescale. The adjudicator should not have his desk cluttered with unnecessary documents or long-winded statements. The statement should be concise, clear and well-argued, setting out the background to the dispute, the contractual position, the dispute, the evidence and arguments which are relevant. Because of the limited timescale, most adjudications will relate to a single issue or a small number of related issues. It should be possible to cover these adequately in a few pages of type, with references to supporting documents.

6.7 Supporting Documents

The referrer should gather documents on which he will rely to demonstrate his case. These will include the contract, or evidence of the contract or agreement, evidence of the nature of the contract works as construction operations in the terms of The Act; letters, architects' instructions, specification and drawings, and any other relevant document.

All of the documents should be listed in date order and numbered, copied and made up as a bundle, with a copy of the document list. Sets should be prepared for the adjudicator and the parties to the dispute. All references to those documents can then be made by using the reference number. Where there is a key passage which is relevant, it should be identified so that the adjudicator will find it easily, by page number, paragraph number and line as appropriate.

Although every useful document should be included, it is important that the bundle should be as compact as possible. Where a large number of documents is found relevant it is usually helpful to make a core bundle of the essentials, and a further bundle for detailed reference if needed.

There is a danger that the adjudicator, faced with a wagon load of lever arch files, might decline to adjudicate on the grounds that the evidence cannot be read and absorbed within the timescale. If very time consuming proof is necessary, he should be asked for a working decision on short evidence, to allow work to proceed, bearing in mind that an unsuccessful party will be able to take full evidence to arbitration or litigation at a later date.

6.8 Requests to the Adjudicator

It is sometimes helpful for a party communicating his case to ask the adjudicator to arrange a site visit, or a meeting, perhaps with witnesses available. A disputant may also ask the adjudicator to obtain legal or expert advice in connection with a particular matter.

A party may wish to be represented by a lawyer or other person to articulate his case. The adjudicator may wish to limit the number of such representatives, or of witnesses.

A party may request the adjudicator to give reasons in his decision. Reasons are discussed below — see 10.2 Reasons behind the Decision

Any request should be made as early as possible in the proceedings so that the adjudicator can arrange times, give the other disputants the opportunity to attend and so on.

The adjudicator, being impartial, will consider any request with a view to satisfying the principles of natural justice — fair hearing of all disputants; opportunity for the disputants to reply in argument; and an equitable balance of opportunity for the disputants. The referrer might have the advantage of timing his Notice of Adjudication but the other parties will be given full opportunity to respond within the available timescale.

6.9 Circulation of copies

All documents and communications between the parties and the adjudicator must be copied simultaneously to the other parties so that everyone is aware of everything that happens and of everything that is presented. In particular, the adjudicator will wish to be satisfied that this equitable arrangement has been maintained.

7. Procedure in the Adjudication

7.1 Box 8 Procedure in the Adjudication

R Day

The Referral Day; the Referrer refers the dispute to the Adjudicator.

SOON The Adjudicator directs the Timetable and Procedure.

SOON The Referrer sends to the Adjudicator and the Other Party:-

A full statement of case,
copies of supporting documents to be relied on,
witness statements to be relied on,
Requests for site visit, tests etc..

SOON The Other Party sends to the Adjudicator & Referrer:-

A full statement of reply,
copies of supporting documents to be relied on,
witness statements to be relied on,
Requests for site visit, tests etc..

The Adjudicator:-

establishes procedure,
establishes a timetable within the timescale,
ascertains the facts and the law,
makes a site visit,
orders tests and opening up as required,
takes legal or technical advice,
questions witnesses,

Within 28 days of Referral the Adjudicator gives his Decision.

Decision Day = D Day = R Day + up to 28 days

Time may be extended:-

D Day = R Day +< 28 days + up to 14 days = up to 42 days

if the Referrer agrees,

D Day = R Day + up to 28 days + *n* days = any length of time

if both parties agree it.

7.2 Adjudicators' Directions

Once he is appointed and has the Notice of Referral and documentation from the Referrer, the adjudicator will take control of the process; he will issue directions to the parties for procedure and will arrange matters so that he may complete his task within the permitted time.

The adjudicator will issue directions to the parties concerning various matters in which he is entitled to demand performance by the parties. His powers are set out in the procedural rules for the particular adjudication. These are usually wide so that he can do anything necessary to obtain relevant information and to make a fair and impartial decision.

7.2.1 Timetable

In any adjudication under the Act, the timescale is of paramount importance.

Within the timescale, the adjudicator will wish to set dates by which various things must happen if he is to reach his decision in time. He will give deadlines for evidence and information. He will arrange meetings and visits. The available time being short, the adjudicator will be unable to allow a dilatory disputant any extra time to get himself organised. The parties may expect to be held to the timetable set by the adjudicator.

7.2.2 Evidence

The adjudicator is impartial. He will receive evidence in any convenient form; by reading documents, by hearing statements and opinions, and by inspection. He is not bound by court rules of evidence and may decide how to regard any evidence presented. He is open to persuasion by any reasonable means. Where evidence conflicts, he may decide which party's evidence he favours on the balance of probability. It is up to the parties to present their evidence effectively.

Where one party decides to pay a lawyer or expert to represent him, the other party, who may have decided to save cost by presenting his own case, might feel at a disadvantage. A trained and experienced adjudicator will ensure that the unrepresented party is not disadvantaged and will take care that he is offered the appropriate opportunities to conduct his case effectively.

The adjudicator has power to ascertain the facts and the law. He may decide to question the parties, or their witnesses. In hearing oral evidence an adjudicator has power to administer oaths so that witnesses speak to him under oath.

7.2.3 Visits

Many contentious issues in construction disputes depend on the adjudicator seeing the evidence so that he can decide how to regard evidence. Although he is likely to be an expert, he will not apply his expert knowledge other than in understanding the evidence concerning the issue. He may take measurements or photographs, or make site notes.

7.2.4 Tests and Experiments

Where material or workmanship is allegedly at fault it may be necessary to arrange for tests or experiments to be conducted. Subject to consent for access and removal of samples, the adjudicator may order tests or experiments. Normally, in arbitration or litigation, the parties each make their own and each provides an expert's interpretation of the results. In order to save time and cost, the parties may ask the adjudicator to arrange his own tests or experiments by an independent third party.

Some tests take time to conduct and may necessarily be completed beyond the time for the decision. In such a case, if the parties do not agree to an extension of time, the adjudicator may be obliged to give a conditional decision, or to say that he cannot decide on the available evidence.

7.3 A Party's Failure to Comply

The Act gives the adjudicator the power to take the initiative in establishing facts and law. The Scheme has typical provisions in exercising this power, and in particular, obliges the parties to comply with the adjudicator's directions. The adjudicator cannot subpoena a party to attend. If a party fails to comply without reasonable cause, the adjudicator has power to move forward to his decision, to continue regardless, to draw adverse inferences, and to use his discretion in considering any late information.

A party cannot hold up the process by failing to follow the adjudicator's directions.

7.4 Expert and Legal Advice

The parties will present the opinions of experts and lawyers in support of their cases. The Act allows the adjudicator to take the initiative to ascertain the facts and the law necessary to determine the dispute. He may obtain advice himself and charge the cost to the parties with his expenses. He should advise the parties that he intends to do this so that they have the opportunity to persuade him otherwise, particularly on grounds of cost, but it remains in his power.

7.5 Facts and Law

In assessing the assembled evidence the adjudicator will seek out the facts and the applicable law. Facts for this purpose may include real, documentary, or oral evidence and opinion. Law includes duty, obligation and right. In order to reach a decision he will find out what are the facts and the law in the particular dispute and then apply the law to the facts.

7.6 Extension of Time

The Act requires a decision to be made within 28 days, or within a further 14 days with the consent of the referrer. In principle, Government intends that the limit should be 42 days. Any other possibility of extension must be a matter of joint agreement between the parties and the rules may accommodate this. The Scheme, at 19.-(1)(c) allows:-

"such period exceeding 28 days after the referral notice as the parties to the dispute may, after the giving of that notice, agree."

Thus, once the Notice of Referral has been given;

— if the referrer needs up to 14 extra days, he can arrange to take them, the adjudicator cannot stop him;

— if the adjudicator or the non-referring party needs an extension of time he may get up to 14 days only if the referrer agrees;

— if the adjudicator or either party needs more that 14 days extension, it will only be possible if the disputants jointly agree.

8. The Response

8.1 Statement of Response

The Act and The Scheme are silent on the actions of the non-referring party. Clearly he will want to defend himself. The response will contest the issues. The adjudicator is required to be impartial. Each point made in the referrer's statement and evidence should be considered by the other parties and answered. Failure to answer the claim will result in the adjudicator's only hearing the referrer's position and the claim may succeed undefended, just as a claim succeeds in court if undefended.

The statement of response will follow the same principles as the referrer's statement and the reader should refer to these as set out above under the heading of *6. The Referrers' Actions in the Adjudication.*

The Notice of Adjudication will have set out the issues in dispute.

The Referral Notice will have engaged an adjudicator to determine the dispute.

The remaining sections should be mirrored in the response.

The Referrer's Statement	- v -	The Response Statement
Supporting Documents	&	Supporting Documents
Requests to the Adjudicator	&	Requests to the Adjudicator
Circulation of copies	&	Circulation of copies

There are additional strategies which the response may include. These are set out below.

8.2 Common Ground

There is no point in trailing the adjudicator across undisputed territory. It serves no purpose and increases the time he spends on the adjudication at the parties' expense. Common ground should be acknowledged at the outset of the response and clearly identified.

8.3 Denial

It is a normal principle of English law that he who asserts must prove. It is important that the writer of a response should understand this principle since the adjudicator will look to him for denial or argument.

The referrer will have made assertions which he must prove to the adjudicator. If the other side simply denies them, the burden of proof still lies on the referrer. However, if there is evidence to be brought by the other side, they may counter the assertions and take on the burden of proving the counter-assertion.

A simple contract may provide for a consideration to be paid promptly on satisfactory completion of a service. To succeed in a claim for payment the contractor has only to prove that there is a contract, that the service has been satisfactorily performed, and that payment is due. If the employer simply denies any of these things, the claimant is still left proving them. If the employer says he will not pay because the work is unsatisfactory he will need to prove the contractor's failure.

8.4 Counterclaim

In legal proceedings and in arbitration it is usual for the defendant or respondent to draw into the dispute other matters to offset against the claim. These may serve to balance the dispute and settle a number of other scores. It must be seen that this is also used as a strategy to obfuscate the matter so that the judge or arbitrator cannot see the crux for the obfuscation.

Counterclaim will rarely be found in adjudication since additional issues can only be raised with the agreement of the referrer and he is hardly likely to admit them to his referral.

9. Additional Issues & Additional Parties

The Act is silent on the subject of additional issues being introduced during adjudication. They are dealt with in some adjudication rules. The basic principle is that the adjudication is called for by the referrer and he has control over what is to be determined. If additional matters are introduced, they will occupy more of the adjudicator's time and will give rise to additional cost which may be allocated against either party. It follows that the parties should be asked for consent to widen the scope of the action. Additions may also affect the timescale for the decision.

9.1 The Parties' Additions

The Scheme, at cl.8, provides that the adjudicator may adjudicate at the same time on one or more disputes under the same contract, with the consent of all of the parties to those disputes. Similarly he may adjudicate at the same time on related disputes under different contracts. As the co-operation of all parties and the adjudicator is needed, it follows that the adjudicator or any of the parties could block the introduction of additional issues.

There will be occasions when a decision in one contract has an effect on a dispute under another contract, and it would be helpful if they can be determined together.

9.2 Others' Additions

Adjudication is a private process involving only the parties to the dispute and the adjudicator. Although other parties to a contract may be affected by an adjudicator's decision, they cannot muscle in on the process. They are free to start a separate adjudication in parallel and there is nothing to stop them from asking if their dispute can be considered at the same time.

9.3 Adjudicator's Opening up, Review and Revisions

There is additional scope for the issues to be widened by the adjudicator, although he will use such power cautiously. He is unlikely to go outside the issues which have been referred to him unless requested by the parties to do so. The Scheme at cl.20 allows him discretion to open up, revise and review any decision or any certificate given by any person referred to in the contract unless it is final and conclusive. Thus an interim certificate for payment or a certificate for extension of time may be changed by the adjudicator's decision. He will decide whether a contract administrator's decision is valid under a contract. He will decide whether work is in accordance with a contract specification. He will not adopt design responsibility by changing the specification or the design.

9.4 Additional Parties

Legal proceedings and arbitration allow joinder of parties, usually on the defending side where more than one party is seen to be at fault, or where the fault is that of a third party outside a contract: the action is pursued against several parties in the hope that the claim will stick somewhere. A multiplicity of parties can extend the time taken in the proceedings since each must have adequate opportunity of a fair hearing.

Neither The Act nor The Scheme mention the possibility of joinder and it is not found in most adjudication procedures other than where notice is served on more than one in a multi-party contract. CICMAP provides at cl.26 that additional parties may be joined if the new and the original parties agree. However, since the adjudicator can only decide issues which arise under the contract, he will not be able to decide matters where they extend beyond the contract, such as sub-contracts or independent contracts. Such situations might be dealt with under parallel adjudications so that the adjudicator can deal with a bunch of related or interdependent matters. The timescale and dates of referral might make this difficult to effect unless the parties agree to co-operate by giving adequate time.

10. The Decision

10.1 Form of the Decision

The decision represents the last step in the adjudication as far as the adjudicator is concerned. Once he has delivered it, his work is finished and it then rests between the parties for action.

It would be sufficient under The Act for the adjudicator to tell the parties what he has decided, or to send a note of it to them.

In practice, the adjudicator will be aware of the use to which his decision might be put and he should structure it accordingly. He will wish to be seen to have conducted the adjudication properly and impartially. In particular, he may include the following:-

- Identity of the contract, form, date, works,
- Identity of the parties to the contract,
- Identity of the parties to the dispute,
- Reference to the Notice of Adjudication, with date,
- Reference to the Referral Notice, with date,
- The Issues as Referred,
- His appointment,
- His jurisdiction under The Act and Rules or Scheme,
- Timescale of the Adjudication,
- Procedure, Orders and Directions,
- List of Documents seen as evidence,
- Outline of Oral Evidence,
- Record of Visits and Inspections,
- Result of Tests,
- External Advice,
- Facts found and Law applied,
- Reasons if called for,
- The Decision, and any Peremptory Orders,

- Orders for Direction of the Parties for payment and action,
- Allocation of Costs.

10.2 Reasons behind the Decision

The Act does not oblige the adjudicator to give the parties reasons behind his decision. He will almost certainly have made notes of his reasons while reaching his decision but he will not be available for any later discussion about his reasoning. The parties are at liberty to ask him for reasons but they should be aware that this would increase the cost of the adjudicator's services. The different procedures give differing weights of obligation for reasons:-

Scheme:- the adjudicator will give reasons if requested to by a party.

JCT:- the adjudicator shall not be obliged to give reasons.

ICE:- the adjudicator shall not be required to give reasons.

CICMAP:- the adjudicator shall not be required to give reasons.

CEDR:- the adjudicator may, but is not obliged to give reasons.

ORSA:- the adjudicator shall not include any reasons.

There are pros and cons in assessing the desirability of stating reasons.

Against stating reasons are the following:-

- the Adjudicator is only paid for his decision;
- he need not give reasons unless asked for them;
- the bald decision gives no rise to argument;
- the adjudicator will not be available to argue anyway;
- there is no mechanism for appeal against an adjudicator's decision;
- if a party is dissatisfied with reasons he must still accept the decision.

For stating reasons are the following:-

- reasons enable the parties, particularly losing parties, to understand how the Adjudicator has come to his decision;

- reasons may help the loser come to terms with loss;
- reasons may give a party an idea for argument and give rise to referral to a higher tribunal where his case will be heard anew;
- if, from the reasons, a party realises how it failed to present its case adequately, it may feel justified in referring to a higher tribunal;
- if the matter is brought to a subsequent tribunal in arbitration or litigation, the reasons may be provided for that tribunal to read when assessing the dispute.

10.3 Communication of the Decision

The Act only requires the adjudicator to decide in order to determine the dispute. The decision could be communicated orally.

The Scheme, at cl.19. (3), determines that as soon as possible after he has reached a decision, the adjudicator shall deliver a copy of that decision to each of the parties to the contract — it will be written and delivered.

Some rules for adjudication provide that the adjudicator may demand payment of his fees and expenses before delivering his decision. In the absence of such a rule most adjudicators will have it as a term of their appointment that they are to have security for the cost of their fees and expenses by stages in advance. This is a normal term for people engaged in contentious work who do not want to have to chase through the courts the people they have helped by determining a dispute. If security is required it will usually be the referrer who pays first in order to have the decision. Costs may be allocated differently—see below under *11.1.4 Apportionment by the Adjudicator*

10.4 Cannot Decide — Provisional and Default Decisions

The Adjudicator's decision that he is unable to decide finally should be made a Decision in the Adjudication. Matters then go to any subsequent procedure in the contract. This is not to say that a Decision can confirm that the Adjudicator cannot make his mind up who to believe. This he must do although he may decide to indicate that both the disputants were closely matched.

The Adjudicator might reasonably decide that he is unable to decide finally, for example:-

- very complex matters, necessitating voluminous evidence which could not be processed in the timescale;
- technical matters requiring long term tests and observations;
- matters requiring external advice which cannot be procured in time.

There also may be circumstances where only a provisional decision is possible, dependent on subsequent events. The Adjudicator might wish to make a Decision conditional on some future event; in this case he would also need a default Decision which would be final.

10.5 Peremptory Orders

A peremptory order is an order in the form of an ultimatum. To be effective it must direct what is to be done, by whom, when or by when, and what will happen in the event of failure to perform. It is usually used after a party has failed to do something and he is given formal notice to do it or suffer specific consequences.

Under The Scheme the Government has introduced peremptory orders at cl.24 by inserting a provision of the Arbitration Act 1996. This has two uses:-

a) The adjudicator, who has directed a party to do something, such as to produce documents, or to attend for questioning, which the party fails to do, may make a peremptory order to the effect that unless it is done within a specific time, the adjudicator will proceed without regard to that information or evidence and may draw adverse inference from the party's failure to perform as directed.

b) If the Decision is made the subject of a peremptory order, the successful party may confidently take it to court for summary enforcement.

10.6 Effect of the Decision

A decision of an adjudicator has the effect of obliging the parties to accept the decision for the time being and to comply with it.

10.6.1 Binding until Determined Otherwise by Arbitration or Litigation

The Act, at s.108. (3) provides that the decision of the adjudicator is binding until it is finally determined otherwise by legal proceedings, by arbitration, or by agreement between the parties.

A dissatisfied party may only get the decision set aside by the court in the event that the adjudicator has acted in bad faith, or shown partiality. Otherwise, if he cannot persuade the other party to agree, the matter must be taken to another tribunal to be heard afresh. Most forms of construction contract include an arbitration clause, the effect of which is to place arbitration as the means of securing binding resolution of disputes, without legal proceedings. The courts take the view that an arbitrator who has determined a dispute did so as contracted and the parties must accept the consequences — the courts have no discretion to interfere.

10.6.2 No Re-adjudication of the Same Issue

A party cannot take the matter on the rounds of adjudicators until he gets the decision he wants. Once a matter is decided by one adjudicator that is the only time it will be decided.

Scheme:- The adjudicator must resign if the dispute has previously been referred and decided.

CICMAP:- No issue decided by an adjudicator may be referred to another adjudicator unless the parties agree to do so.

ICE :- No issue previously decided by an adjudicator may be laid before another adjudicator unless the parties agree.

Since a new adjudicator will not know the history, all the above provisions rely on the other party to blow a whistle if a matter is re-referred to another adjudicator.

10.6.3 Binding by Default of Complaint

The Act provides that the parties may decide to agree to be bound by the decision. Such a decision, properly recorded, will stop further action if a party later has second thoughts.

Some rules for adjudication provide that if a party does not give notice of dissatisfaction within a set period, such as two months, the decision becomes finally binding by default. This provision is not included in The Scheme so in an adjudication under The Scheme, the party can only take the dispute to another tribunal.

10.6.4 Directed Action of Parties

The actions which an adjudicator can order are limited. He can decide whether things are in accordance with the contract. Under The Scheme, he can decide to revise decisions or certificates given by a person who is named in the contract; he can decide payment under the contract (not damages, which are outside the contract). He can decide interest at his own discretion. ICE makes the same provision but JCT only allows interest to be decided if interest accrues under the terms of the contract.

To take an example:- where an architect has rejected a wall as badly built and has instructed that it be taken down and rebuilt, and the contractor feels that the wall is satisfactory, the adjudicator can decide whether the wall is in accordance with the specification and drawings, whether the architect has power to have it rebuilt in any case, and who should bear the cost of rebuilding. He cannot instruct the contractor to rebuild the wall.

10.6.5 Time for Action

The Scheme at cl.23. (2) determines that the parties must comply with the adjudicator's decision. cl.21 provides that if no time is stated, the parties must comply immediately on delivery of the Decision. The adjudicator should decide and state a reasonable time for compliance and make this enforceable by making a peremptory order.

10.6.6 Failure to Act

If a party fails to do as directed, whether payment or action, the other party can only take enforcement action through the court.

10.6.7 Enforcement of Action

Enforcement is the process by which a successful party can force the other party to comply with an adjudicator's directions. Enforcement is not specifically covered by The Act, which relies on the dispute being taken to a fresh and higher tribunal.

The Scheme, in providing for peremptory orders, at cl.24, enables the successful party to have such orders summarily enforced at court. The mechanism is taken from selected parts of s.42 of The Arbitration Act 1996 which provides that unless otherwise agreed by the parties, the court may make an order requiring a party to comply with a peremptory order made by the adjudicator. The application to the court may be made by the adjudicator (only during the adjudication) or by a party to the adjudication with the permission of the adjudicator (and upon notice to the other parties). The last provision is odd since the Adjudicator has given a decision and is finished. It seems likely that the courts might summarily enforce the decision without any involvement of the Adjudicator.

The court must be satisfied that the person to whom the adjudicator's order was directed has failed to comply with it within the time prescribed in the order or, if no time was prescribed, within a reasonable time. The leave of the court is required for any appeal from a decision of the court under this provision.

The court will not review the order, nor look at the reasons behind it. It will summarily bind the party by an order of the court to comply in the terms of the adjudicator's order. This has the effect of making the adjudicator's order into a court order which if not obeyed could result in imprisonment for contempt of court.

11. Costs

There are two categories of costs:- the costs of the adjudication, and party costs. These are defined below. In legal and arbitration proceedings the successful party can usually apply for his costs to be paid by the unsuccessful party and an order is made to that effect. In adjudication, there is no provision for party costs to be allocated.

11.1 The Adjudicator's Costs

These are the costs of the adjudication itself.

11.1.1 Fees and Expenses

Since the Adjudicator is appointed on being sent the Referral Notice, and is entitled to his reasonable fees and expenses he may decide to proceed without any other agreement feeling secure in a contract which arises from the Scheme. Most Adjudicators might wish to apply their own standard terms and conditions to their appointment, setting out their rates for time and expenses, period for payment and any charges or interest for delayed payment. In accordance with common practice in contentious work they might require the security of payment into their client account in advance of proceeding. They may also wish to make it a term that they are indemnified by the Parties against any liability to third parties which may arise out of the adjudication. Such terms should be notified to the parties immediately upon becoming aware of the intended referral so that there can be no doubt about the Adjudicator's terms from the outset.

By the appointment of an adjudicator, the parties form a contract with him and he is entitled to be paid reasonable fees and to recover expenses reasonably incurred. An adjudicator will usually confirm his hourly or daily rates prior to appointment and require acceptance of them at least by the referrer before accepting the appointment. Adjudicator's rates are likely to be similar to those of arbitrators and of lawyers in the particular locality.

The adjudicator's expenses may include travel and subsistence, meeting room rent, telephone, photography and copying, and the cost of advice or tests or opening up which he has commissioned. These items are normally charged at cost as disbursed by the adjudicator.

Adjudications administered by an organisation such as CEDR may also be subject to arrangement fees. CEDR adjudication charges reflect London rates.

11.1.2 Cost of Advice, Tests etc.

Under the Act, the adjudicator has the power to take the initiative in ascertaining the facts and the law, and he may need to take advice from experts or lawyers. He may also need to arrange tests or experiments. The Scheme, at 13 (e) enables him to arrange tests or experiments subject to obtaining consent from third parties, and (f) enable him to appoint experts, assessors or legal advisers provided he has first notified the parties. The cost of such arrangements and advice will be treated as a disbursement and recovered from the parties with his other expenses.

If a party objects to spending money in this way he should make representations to the adjudicator, who may either go ahead anyway on the grounds that the advice is necessary for him to determine the matter, or make a decision based on the limited information already to hand.

As a matter of strategy for the parties, if the parties commission their own experts, they will not be able to recover the cost. If the adjudicator commissions them, the cost may be allocated.

11.1.3 Liability for Payment

The Act is silent on the payment of the adjudicator. He may make a term of his appointment that the parties are to pay half each in advance. He will also make the parties jointly and severally liable which means that he can, if necessary collect all of his charges from either party in the case of one party defaulting on payment. Alternatively he may demand payment in advance by the referrer and leave it open for a claim for apportioned costs to be allocated following the result of the adjudication. A party wishing the other party to bear the costs of the arbitration should ask the adjudicator to apportion them after reaching his decision on the substantive issues.

11.1.4 Apportionment by the Adjudicator

It is normal in legal proceedings and in arbitration that the court can order an unsuccessful party to bear some or all the costs of the successful party. The Act does not make any provision for the adjudicator to apportion liability for costs differently between the parties and such provision would need to be made in the particular contract rules. The Scheme makes the parties jointly and severally liable for any sum which remains outstanding of his reasonable fees and expenses following the making of any determination on how the payment shall be apportioned. Thus, under the Scheme the adjudicator may see fit to allocate costs against a losing party.

11.1.5 Time for Payment

Neither the Act nor the Scheme give any particular time for payment of the adjudicator; it is left to him to make commercial arrangements under his own terms of appointment. Most adjudicators will follow the convention in contentious work and will ask to be paid in advance by stages, receiving funds periodically into his client account which he will draw down periodically on preparation of invoices based on time spent and expenses disbursed. Failing such an arrangement an adjudicator would expect prompt and full payment on demand and would not expect to have to chase the disputants through the courts after he has determined their dispute.

11.2 The Parties' Costs

The parties may decide to appoint experts or lawyers to assist or represent them. These are party costs which they incur individually in addition to their own overhead costs of preparing statements and administering their cases.

11.2.1 Apportionment by the Adjudicator

Although judges and arbitrators have power to allocate the successful claimant's party costs against a losing party, there is no such provision in adjudication, and unless the parties jointly agree to ask the adjudicator to allocate party costs, he will not be involved with them.

11.2.2 Party Basis

In the absence of differential allocation of party costs they must be settled on a party basis; each party pays the costs individually incurred.

12. Liability of the Adjudicator

The adjudicator's duty is to the parties to the adjudication and he contracts with them to do his work in accordance with the law.

In undertaking to determine a dispute impartially and to the best of his ability, an adjudicator does not want to be seen to be putting his head above the parapet to be shot or taken hostage by the disputants or by anyone else.

12.1 Liability to the Parties

12.1.1 Good Faith / Bad Faith

If someone acts impartially and fairly for a reasonable cost he is acting in good faith. This is the state of the parties at the outset of any commercial contract or equitable agreement.

The Act at s.108.(4) provides that:-

"The contract shall also provide that the adjudicator is not liable for anything done or omitted in the discharge or purported discharge of his functions as adjudicator unless the act or omission is in bad faith."

This provision is taken up in the various rules for adjudication. Bad faith is wider than the opposite of good faith. Bad faith covers prejudice, partiality, malice, corruption and fraud, but it does not cover innocent mistake or simple negligence.

The adjudicator who does his honest best will not incur liability for a mistake, although he might be expected to correct the mistake.

12.1.2 Impartiality

The Act provides that the contract shall impose a duty on the adjudicator to act impartially. This duty is reproduced in the schemes of rules. Impartially means free of prejudice or bias. This may be seen as the paramount quality in an adjudicator. He will not only act impartially, he will avoid any position in which his partiality may be questioned. He will not act if he has a prior business or personal relationship with one of the parties and he may be expected to declare any acquaintance beyond the purely professional.

12.1.3 Initiative in Ascertaining Facts and Law

The Act provides that a contract shall enable the adjudicator to take the initiative in ascertaining the facts and the law. This is expressed as a power rather than a duty. The adjudication is time limited and is not an inevitably binding process so the adjudicator will exercise this power to the extent that time and professional good sense allow. He will not be liable if he decides not to pursue some evidence relentlessly, or to find an obscure point of law.

12.2 Liability of the Adjudicator to Others

It is possible that the adjudicator's decision might have an adverse effect on third parties such as sub-contractors, suppliers or neighbours, who might be inclined to pursue him. It is necessary to understand that his adjudication is concerned only with matters under a particular contract between the disputants and it only determines issues within that contract. Any external effect of the contract is a matter for the parties, and not for the adjudicator.

Nevertheless, some rules do attempt to set out the immunity of the adjudicator from third party claims. ICE 7.2 includes the following:-

"The Parties shall save harmless and indemnify the Adjudicator and any employee or agent of the Adjudicator against all claims by third parties and in respect of this shall be jointly and severally liable."

The adjudicator may decide to include a similar clause in his terms of engagement, taking the view that he should make it clear that he is there only to determine a dispute, not to incur or adopt liability.

In providing for statutory adjudication Government and the construction industry do not expect the Adjudicator to take on any liability from disputants; the Adjudicator should be in the same immune position as a judge or an arbitrator.

Appendix A — The Housing Grants, Construction and Regeneration Act

For the purposes of adjudication, The Housing Grants, Construction and Regeneration Act 1996 became effective on 1 May 1998 with the publication of the related Scheme for Construction Contracts. The Act is SI 1998/650 and adjudication is found in Part II, Construction Contracts. Part II applies in England and Wales, Scotland and Northern Ireland

Note that except for S.108, the text of The Act is not reproduced here. The following commentary gives an outline of the provisions of The Act Section by Section.

S. 104 Construction Contracts

A construction contract is defined as an agreement with a person — for, arranging for, or providing the labour, or the labour of others for — the carrying out of construction operations. (Construction operations and agreements are defined later.)

A construction contract in this part also includes an agreement to do architectural, design, or surveying work, or to provide advice on building, engineering, interior or exterior decoration, or landscape laying out, in relation to construction operations.

Note that not only is the builder's work under a construction contract, but also the work of the professional design team members. The architect making a feasibility study for a building is a party to a construction contract with his client.

Construction contracts do not include contracts of employment.

If the agreement relates both to construction operations and other matters the above provisions apply only to the construction work.

Only contracts entered into on or after 1 May 98 are affected.

S. 105 Construction Operations

There follows a very widely defined list of construction operations including almost all of the works which are usually included in a contractor's work, from excavation to decoration and communications systems, landscaping, repairs and demolition.

Subsection (2) lists excluded operations. The text of S.105.-(2) follows:-

(2) The following operations are not construction operations within the meaning of this Part-

(a) drilling for, or extraction of, oil or natural gas;

(b) extraction (whether by underground or surface working) of minerals; tunnelling or boring, or construction of underground works, for this purpose;

(c) assembly, installation or demolition of plant or machinery, or erection or demolition of steelwork for the purposes of supporting or providing access to plant or machinery, on a site where the primary activity is-

(i) nuclear processing, power generation, or water or effluent treatment, or

(ii) the production, transmission, processing or bulk storage (other than warehousing) of chemicals, pharmaceuticals, oil, gas, steel or food and drink;

(d) manufacture or delivery to site of-

(i) building or engineering components or equipment,

(ii) materials, plant or machinery, or

(iii) components for systems of heating, lighting, air-conditioning, ventilation, power supply, drainage, sanitation, water supply or fire protection, or for security or communications systems,

except under a contract which also provides for their installation;

(e) the making, installation and repair of artistic works, being sculptures, murals and other works which are wholly artistic in nature.

See also the Exclusion Order at Appendix B

S. 106 Some Residential Works excluded

Here there is a narrow definition of works which are excluded because the work principally relates to operations on a dwelling which is, or is to be, the residence of a party to the contract. To qualify for this exclusion the dwelling may be a house or a flat; but if a house, it must not contain a flat; if a flat, it is to be separate and self contained and divided horizontally from other parts of the premises.

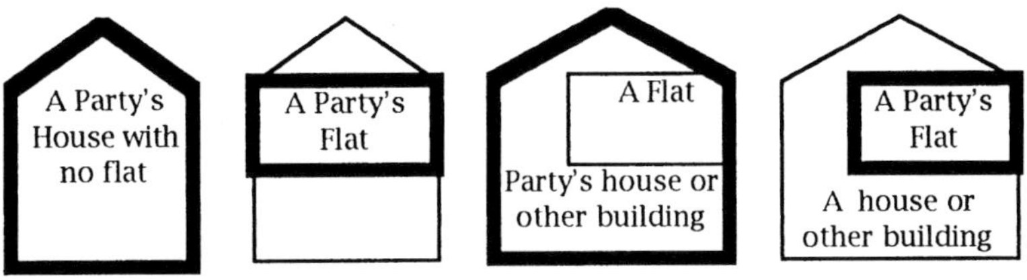

Single dwelling is excluded only if it is an isolated or horizontally divided dwelling of a Party.

Neither dwelling is excluded as the house or other building contains a flat not horizontally divided.

The wording here is rather tortuous and needs careful scrutiny if the exclusion is to be warranted.

S. 107 Agreements in Writing or Recorded by Other Means

The construction contract must be:-

- made in writing;
- by an exchange of written communication;
- evidenced in writing;
- other than in writing but by reference to terms which are in writing;
- recorded by a party or a third party with authority;
- recorded by any other means.

Written submissions in adjudication, arbitration or litigation under an unwritten agreement, in which the agreement is not denied, also form written acknowledgement of an agreement.

S. 108 Adjudication

This is the Section which introduces the right to refer a dispute to adjudication and all statutory adjudication in construction contracts springs from this Section and is subject to its provisions. I reproduce the main part in full. My comments are underlined.

108.-(1) A party to a construction contract has the right to refer a dispute arising under the contract for adjudication under a procedure complying with this section.

<u>Any party has a unilateral right to refer</u>

For this purpose "dispute" includes any difference.

<u>any difference</u>

(2) The contract shall--

(a) enable a party to give notice at any time of his intention to refer a dispute to adjudication;

'any time' enables ambush

(b) provide a timetable with the object of securing the appointment of the adjudicator and referral of the dispute to him within 7 days of such notice;

Object of Appointment within 7 days

(c) require the adjudicator to reach a decision within 28 days of referral or such longer period as is agreed by the parties after the dispute has been referred;

to decide within 28 days

(d) allow the adjudicator to extend the period of 28 days by up to 14 days, with the consent of the party by whom the dispute was referred;

or extend up to 14 days by consent

(e) impose a duty on the adjudicator to act impartially;

Impartial Adjudicator

(f) enable the adjudicator to take the initiative in ascertaining the facts and the law.

Ascertains facts and law

(3) The contract shall provide that the decision of the adjudicator is binding until the dispute is finally determined by legal proceedings; by arbitration if the contract provides for arbitration or the

parties otherwise agree to arbitration; or by agreement.

Binding until found or agreed otherwise

The parties may agree to accept the decision of the adjudicator as finally determining the dispute.

Parties may agree to accept

(4) The contract shall also provide that the adjudicator is not liable for anything done or omitted in the discharge or purported discharge of his functions as adjudicator unless the act or omission is in bad faith, and that any employee or agent of the adjudicator is similarly protected from liability.

Adjudicator not liable except in bad faith

(5) If the contract does not comply with the requirements of subsections (1) to (4), the adjudication provisions of The Scheme for Construction Contracts apply.

Contract must comply or The Scheme applies

S. 109 to S. 113 Payment

Sections 109 to 113 give the right of regular payment under all construction contracts. This is not the subject of this guide.

S. 114 Provision of a Default Scheme of Rules

The Scheme for Construction Contracts is provided to apply by default if the contract does not comply with S.108 (1) to (4). See Appendix C

S. 115 Service of Notices, &c.

The parties are free to agree how notices, written communications and documents are to be served. Otherwise service may be by any effective means and either the last known address or registered office address is effective. Note that post must be stamped to be effective, but need not be by recorded delivery. Current practice is to copy a document by fax to establish a date, and to send immediately by 1st Class post.

S. 116 Reckoning Time and Dates

Periods of time begin immediately after a given date; for something to be done within seven days, day 1 is tomorrow and it must be done by the end of day 7.

Only Christmas Day, Good Friday and Bank Holidays are excluded from the calculation of periods expressed in days.

S. 117 The Crown

The provisions apply to the Crown and the Duchy of Cornwall, except for The Queen acting privately.

Appendix B — The Construction Contracts Exclusion Order

Introduced as Statutory Instrument 1998 No. 648, The Construction Contracts (England and Wales) Exclusion Order 1998 amends The Act by excluding certain categories of work.

Note that the provision for Scotland is similar:- Statutory Instrument 1998 No. 686 (S.33) The Construction Contracts (Scotland) Exclusion Order 1998.

The following comments relate to the England and Wales Order.

The following commentary summarises the provisions of the Order, with notes. Reference to the full text should be made before relying on this commentary.

Agreements under Statute

Note that the adjudication provisions are in Part II of The Act.

A construction contract is excluded from the operation of Part II of The Act if it is under:-

S.38 of the Highways Act 1980 (power to adopt by agreement),

S.278 of the Highways Act 1980 (agreement to execution of works),

S.106, S.106A of the Town and Country Planning Act 1990 (obligations),

S.229A of the Town and Country Planning Act 1990 (Crown obligation),

S.104 of the Water Industries Act 1991(power to adopt sewer etc.),

S.1 of the National Health Service (Private Finance) Act 1997.

Agreements under PFI

A construction contract is excluded from the operation of Part II of The Act if it is an agreement under the private finance initiative as specifically defined.

Agreements under Finance or Development Agreements

A construction contract is excluded from the operation of Part II of The Act if it is a finance agreement or development agreement as specifically defined.

Appendix C — The Scheme for Construction Contracts

Introduced as a Statutory Instrument 1998 No. 649 The Scheme for Construction Contracts (England and Wales) Regulations 1998 is in the form of a Schedule of which Part I deals with Adjudication.

Note that the provision for Scotland is similar:-

The Scheme for Construction Contracts (Scotland) Regulations 1998 No. 687 (S.34).

The following comments relate to the England and Wales Scheme.

The Scheme is effective under the Housing Grants, Construction and Regeneration Act 1996 Part II and applies to agreements for construction operations and related professional services agreements entered after 1 May 1998

It is the default scheme of rules which must be used for the resolution of all disputes referred for adjudication if the contract does not contain or specify rules which comply with The Act. The Act rules The Scheme. The Scheme may cover other topics but any requirement of The Act will apply.

Where periods are allowed for certain actions to be made these are in days as defined in The Act S.116 which excludes only Christmas Day, Good Friday and Bank Holidays.

The following commentary summarises the provisions of The Scheme, with notes. Reference to the full text should be made before relying on this commentary.

Notice of Intention

1.- (1) Any party, as the Referring Party, gives a Notice of Adjudication

(2) to every other party to the contract

(3) setting out briefly

(a) the nature & brief description of dispute and parties involved,

(b) details where & when it has arisen,

(c) redress which is sought,

(d) names and addresses of Parties to the Contract.

Note that parties to the dispute may not be all of the parties to the contract. The contract parties are all informed of the dispute but only the dispute parties take part in the adjudication.

Selecting the Adjudicator

2.- (1) Then:-

(a) the adjudicator named in the contract is requested to act

or (b) if no-one is named, or the named person cannot act, the nominating body named is requested to select the adjudicator

or (c) if neither (a) nor (b), a nominating body selects the adjudicator.

There are pros and cons to being named in contracts. Adjudicators who make themselves available by accepting nomination in contracts must be ready to take up Referrals if they arise. On the other hand a Referral may arise which, for example, needs an engineer-adjudicator where an architect has been named. The architect must decide whether it is reasonable to decline the Referral, leaving the opportunity open for an engineer, or to accept and to be prepared to take advice from an engineer at the expense of the parties.

The RIBA, like other professional institutions maintains a panel of selected and monitored adjudicators from which to select a name on request as an Adjudicator Nominating Body. DOE will maintain a list of such bodies.

(2) Within 2 days of receiving a request the adjudicator indicates willingness to act.

(3) An adjudicator nominating body is one which holds itself out as such.

This last provision has inherent dangers. There is no governmental system of vetting the adjudicator nominating bodies, or the people who they nominate. In the interest of consumer protection the Construction Industry Council is co-ordinating the nominating function of CIC constituent bodies to ensure that their nominated adjudicators are trained and monitored to a common standard. CEDR and ORSA have their own monitoring system.

Appointing the Adjudicator

3.- The Notice of Adjudication accompanies the request to the adjudicator to act.

4.- The adjudicator is to be a disinterested "natural" person, i.e.: not a firm, nor a person affected by the decision.

5.- (1) Within 5 days of receiving a request a nominating body must select an adjudicator.

(2) If a nominating body fails to select within 5 days the Referring Party

(a) agrees a name with the other parties to the dispute

or (b) requests any other adjudicator nominating body to select an adjudicator.

(3) Within 2 days of receiving a request the adjudicator indicates willingness to act.

6.- (1) If the adjudicator named in the contract is unwilling or unable or does not respond,

then 6.-(1)(a) (b) (c) and (2) operate like section 2 above.

7.- (1) Within 7 days of Notice of Adjudication, referral is made by sending the Referral Notice

(2) with copies or extracts from the contract, and documents relied on, to the adjudicator

(3) at the same time to every other party to the dispute,

Note that the periods in this section can only be objective, not mandatory, since the effective appointment of the adjudicator requires selection, confirmation of willingness to act, and agreement of terms and any of these can cause delay.

Limits to the Adjudicator's Jurisdiction

8.- (1) Multiple adjudications at the same time, on the same contract, with disputants' consent.

(2) Related adjudications at the same time, on other contracts, with disputants' consent.

(3) Adjudication timescale can be extended by all party agreement.

(4) Adjudicator displaced by a multiple adjudicator is to be paid.

9.- (1) Adjudicator may resign at any time on written notice to the disputants.

(2) Adjudicator must resign if the dispute has previously been referred and decided,

(3) Where Adjudicator ceases under 9.-(1) to act,

(a) Referrer may repeat 1 to 7 above to get a new adjudication,

(b) new Adjudicator gets copies of all documents sent to predecessor.

(4) Where Adjudicator ceases under 9.-(2) above,

or if a dispute is varied and comes out of Adjudicator's competence,

the Parties must pay him, as he may apportion, jointly and severally liable.

It appears that if he resigns under 9(1) he may not be paid.

10.- A Party's objection to an appointment does not invalidate the appointment nor his decision.

The Adjudicator will not be unseated by a party who dislikes him.

11.- (1) The Parties may agree to revoke the appointment at any time

and the Parties must pay him, jointly and severally liable,

as he may apportion,

(2) but if revocation is due to his default or misconduct, they are not liable.

Powers of the Adjudicator

12.- The Adjudicator shall:-

(a) act impartially, in accordance with the contract, and the law,

(b) avoid incurring unnecessary expense.

13.- The Adjudicator may take the initiative in ascertaining facts and law, and shall decide the procedure in the adjudication, particularly he may:-

(a) request documents, statements and previously copied documents under 7(2);

(b) decide language and whether translation is required;

(c) meet and question parties and their representatives;

(d) make visits and inspections subject to 3rd party consent for access, alone or accompanied;

(e) carry out tests or experiments subject to 3rd party consent for access;

(f) obtain representations and submissions, and,

after notifying the Parties, appoint experts, assessors or legal advisers;

(g) direct timetable, deadlines, and length of documents or oral representations;

(h) direct conduct of the adjudication.

14.- The Parties shall comply with any request or direction of the adjudicator.

Note that 21 provides for immediate compliance and under 23 the Adjudicator may make peremptory orders which are enforceable in court under 24.

15.- If without sufficient cause a party fails to comply, the adjudicator may:-

(a) continue regardless;

(b) draw adverse inferences;

(c) decide how to regard evidence provided outside his directed timescales.

16.- (1) Unless agreed otherwise, any Party may chose assistants, advisers or representatives

but (2) only one to give oral evidence or representation, unless the Adjudicator directs otherwise.

17.- All relevant information provided or obtained by the Adjudicator shall be considered and must be made available to all.

Note that no rules of evidence apply.

18.- Confidential information shall not be disclosed outside the adjudication.

19.- (1) The Adjudicator shall give his Decision not later than:-

(a) 28 days after Referral Notice [7(1) above],

or (b) 42 days after Referral Notice if Referrer consents,

or (c) a longer period agreed between the disputant Parties.

(2) Where the Adjudicator fails to give a decision within those times:-

(a) any Party may serve a fresh Notice of Adjudication starting 1 to 8 again, and

(b) on request, all previous documents are to be supplied to the new Adjudicator.

(3) As soon as possible after his decision the Adjudicator must deliver a copy to each of the contract Parties.

Note that the requirement for a copy implies that the decision will be communicated in writing and will not be held by the adjudicator while he awaits payment.

Adjudicator's Decision

20.- The Adjudicator shall decide the matters in dispute

and any additional matters introduced and agreed by the disputant Parties

or which the Adjudicator considers are necessarily connected,

Particularly he may:-

(a) open up, review and revise any decision or certificate given by a person named in the contract, unless it is stated in the contract to be final and conclusive;

(b) decide a party is liable to make payment, when due and by when;

(c) decide circumstances, rates and periods for interest.

The option of opening up, reviewing and revising any related contractual decision is powerful. He will probably only use it where he considers that matters have been particularly badly served by a decision in the contract. He will not re-design.

Note also that payment directions must comply with The Act.

21.- If no time is directed, Parties must comply immediately on delivery of the Decision.

22.- If requested by one of the disputant Parties the Adjudicator shall give reasons for his decision.

If the matter is brought to a subsequent tribunal in arbitration or litigation, the reasons may be submitted to that tribunal for consideration in assessing the dispute.

Effects of the Decision

23.- (1) The Adjudicator may make peremptory orders in his decision.

A peremptory order is one which is in the form of an ultimatum to perform an action by a given date failing which other action will follow — see cl.24.

(2) The Decision is binding and must be complied with until determined otherwise in arbitration or legal proceeding, or by agreement by the Parties.

If an arbitration clause is omitted from the contract the matter may go straight to legal proceedings.

24.- Section 42 of the Arbitration Act 1996 shall apply with modifications.

The following is a transcription from the Arbitration Act, modified as specified, with headings.

"Powers of court in relation to {adjudication} proceedings

Enforcement of peremptory orders of {adjudicator}

42.- (1) Unless otherwise agreed by the parties, the court may make an order requiring a party to comply with a peremptory order made by the tribunal.

(2) An application for an order under this section may be made-

(a) by the adjudicator (upon notice to the parties),

(b) by a party to the adjudication with the permission of the adjudicator (and upon notice to the other parties), or

(c) deleted.

(3) deleted.

(4) No order shall be made under this section unless the court is satisfied that the person to whom the tribunal's order was directed has failed to comply with it within the time prescribed in the order or, if no time was prescribed, within a reasonable time.

(5) The leave of the court is required for any appeal from a decision of the court under this section."

This section brings in provision for peremptory orders to be enforced by summary judgement of the court. Provided the order is properly made, the court will give automatic enforcement without any review. References to "tribunal" are intended to refer to the Adjudicator.

25 The Adjudicator is entitled to determine payment of his reasonable fees and expenses,

in proportions determined by the Adjudicator,

the Parties being liable jointly and severally for any amount remaining outstanding.

This clause indicates that the Adjudicator may apportion payment of his costs. As there is no indication in The Scheme whether he can decide about costs of the Parties, it should be assumed they bear their own costs. If a Party obtains expert opinion to present to the Adjudicator the cost will be a party cost and the Party must pay for it. But if the Adjudicator obtains advice from an expert under 13(f) that will be a cost of the Adjudication and may be apportioned under 25. This may affect party strategy.

Since the Adjudicator is appointed on being sent the Referral Notice, and is entitled to his reasonable fees and expenses, he may decide to proceed without any other agreement feeling secure in a contract which arises from The Scheme. Most Adjudicators might wish to apply their own standard terms and conditions to their appointment.

26.- The Adjudicator is not liable for anything done or omitted in the adjudication, except in bad faith and his employees or agents are similarly protected.

Appendix D — JCT Adjudication Rules

The Joint Contracts Tribunal publishes a number of standard forms of contract for construction works. These incorporate references for arbitration to take precedence before litigation in the resolution of disputes arising under JCT contracts. The arbitration clause can be optionally struck out.

As a result of The Act adjudication is the mandatory first step to resolution of a dispute arising under the contract. The adjudication clause should not be struck out as the statutory right to adjudication will remain in force. Striking out the adjudication clause would have the effect of making any dispute fall for adjudication under the Government's Scheme for Construction Contracts by default.

The most commonly used JCT Contracts are the Standard Forms of Building Contract 1980 Edition (JCT 80) in versions With, and Without, Quantities and adjudication is included there at a new Article 5 and a new clause 41A which was introduced as part of JCT80 Amendment 18, to be effective with The Act from 1 May 1998. Article 7A and 41B deals with arbitration (optional) and Article 7B and clause 41C with legal proceedings.

Article 5 and clause 41A are used with two alternative forms for the JCT Adjudication Agreement, depending whether the adjudicator is to be named in the contract or not. Following the preference of the industry at large, the standard form is written to be used without a named adjudicator, an appropriate adjudicator being chosen when the dispute has arisen.

If an adjudicator is to be named, it is necessary to make the standard alterations provided for clauses 1.3, 41A.2, 41A.3, and at the Appendix where the name and address are to be inserted with the fee as a lump sum or as an hourly rate.

A similar clause to 41A is included in the other JCT forms of contract although the numbering varies.

The following commentary summarises the provisions of the JCT Rules, with notes. Reference to the full text should be made before relying on this commentary.

JCT 41A Adjudication

Application of 41A

41A.1 41A applies where either party refers any dispute or difference arising under the contract following Article 5.

Identity of Adjudicator

41A.2 The Adjudicator shall be an individual

either agreed by the parties,

or on application by a party, nominated by the nominator named in the Appendix,

Providing that:-

41A.2 .1 the Adjudicator must be willing to enter a JCT Adjudication Agreement;

41A.2 .2 where a party has given notice of intention to refer a dispute to adjudication, then

any agreement has the objective of appointing the adjudicator within 7 days and

any application to the nominator has the same objective;

41A2 .3 on agreement or nomination, the parties shall execute the JCT Adjudication Agreement with the Adjudicator.

Death or Inability of the Adjudicator

41A.3 If the Adjudicator dies or is unavailable, the appointment cycle of 41A.2 is repeated.

Notice of Intention and Referral

41A4 .1 A Party gives notice to the other Party of intention to refer a dispute to adjudication,

and within 7 days from the date of the notice,

or if later, of the execution of the Adjudication Agreement,

makes the referral to the Adjudicator with:-

particulars of the dispute,

a summary of contentions on which he relies,

a statement of the relief or remedy sought,

and any other material to be considered;

and simultaneously sends copies of all this to the other Party.

41A4 .2 The referral and the copies shall be sent:-

by actual delivery,

or by fax, followed by 1st class post or actual delivery,

or by registered post or recorded delivery, post being deemed to arrive within 48 hours of the date of posting, excluding Sundays and Bank Holidays.

Conduct of the Adjudication

41A.5 .1 Immediately on receipt of the referral and accompanying documentation, the Adjudicator shall notify the parties of the date of receipt.

Note that time is of the essence if the adjudication is to be completed within the time limits set by The Act and everyone concerned should be aware of the critical dates. For JCT it is the date of receipt by the adjudicator which starts the clock for the adjudication leading to a Decision within the time allowed.

41A.5 .2 Within 7 days of the date of receipt by the adjudicator, the other party may send, by the same means, to the Adjudicator, and copy to the referrer:-

a written statement of the contentions on which he relies,

and any other material he wishes the Adjudicator to consider.

41A.5 .3 Within 28 days of receipt of the Referral and its accompanying documentation,

acting neither as an expert, nor as an arbitrator,

the Adjudicator shall reach his decision and

forthwith send the decision in writing to the Parties, but

the Referrer may allow the Adjudicator to extend 14 more days

or after referral, the Parties may jointly agree a longer period.

41A.5 .4 The Adjudicator shall not be obliged to give reasons for his decision.

Note that he may be asked to give reasons and may agree to do so. Since it will take time to write reasons he should not be expected to give them without a request, and under this rule he may decline.

41A.5 .5 In reaching his decision, the Adjudicator shall act impartially

and may, at his own discretion:-

set his own procedure,

take the initiative in ascertaining facts and law including:-

41A.5.5 .1 use his own knowledge and experience;

.2 open up, review and revise

any certificate, opinion, decision, requirement, or notice

issued, given, or made under the Contract,

as though it had not been;

.3 require from the Parties, any further information or results of tests or of opening up;

.4 require the Parties to carry out tests or opening up;

.5 visit the site or any workshop;

.6 obtain information from their employees or representatives

providing he gives prior notice to the Party;

.7 subject to giving prior notice and an estimate of cost,

obtain technical information or advice from others;

.8 under the terms of the contract,

decide circumstances and period for simple interest payable.

41A.5 .6 The decision will not be invalidated by failure of a Party

to enter the Adjudication Agreement,

nor to comply with the Adjudicator's requirements under 41A.5.5.

41A.5 .7 The Parties shall meet their own costs

except that the Adjudicator may decide who pays costs of opening up or tests under 41A.5.5.4

Note that the Parties own costs are their costs in bringing the matter to the Adjudicator, including their lawyers, advisers' charges and the cost of their own tests or opening up. They are not the costs in fees, expenses or disbursements by the Adjudicator.

Payment of the Adjudicator

41A.6 .1 The Adjudicator shall decide the apportionment of his fees and expenses between the parties,

but, if he does not do so, the Parties bear the cost equally.

41A.6 .2 The Parties are jointly and severally liable for the Adjudicator's fees and expenses.

Note that the effect here is that although the Adjudicator may decide who should pay what proportion of his costs, if one party defaults on payment, the other must pay all to the Adjudicator.

Effect of the Decision

41A.7 .1 the Decision is binding on the Parties until

either it is decided otherwise in arbitration or litigation,

or the Parties jointly agree otherwise in writing.

41A.7 .2 The Parties shall comply with the Decision and ensure that it is given effect.

Note that Adjudication provides an immediate working decision for the short term.

41A.7 .3 If either Party does not comply with the Decision,

the other Party can secure compliance by legal proceedings independently of any final determination.

Note that this enables the other Party to take the Decision before a judge for summary enforcement. Provided the Decision is written in appropriate terms, stating what is to be done or paid, by whom, to whom, when, by when, and that the other Party can show that it has not been complied with, then the court will issue an order for compliance without looking into the merits of the Adjudicator's Decision. Failure to comply with a court order is a contempt and could result in imprisonment.

Immunity of the Adjudicator

41A.8 The Adjudicator is not liable for anything done or omitted in the adjudication, except in bad faith and his employees or agents are similarly protected.

Appendix E — ICE Adjudication Procedure

The Institution of Civil Engineers' Adjudication Procedure 1997 is principally for use with the ICE family of Conditions of Contract. It is available for other contracts for which it might be suitable although consideration would need to be given to amending the relationship with the ICE Adjudicator's Agreement and the ICE as a nominating body.

The following commentary summarises the provisions of the ICE Adjudication Procedure, with notes. Reference to the full text should be made before relying on this commentary.

General Procedure

1.1 The edition of the ICE Adjudication Procedure current at the time of the Notice of Adjudication is to be used,

and the ICE Adjudicator Agreement is used for the appointment

and in any conflict between the contract and the Procedure, the procedure prevails.

1.2 The object of adjudication under this procedure is to reach a fair, rapid and inexpensive determination of a dispute arising under a contract and the procedure shall be interpreted accordingly.

1.3 The Adjudicator is a named individual

and acts impartially.

Note that an adjudicator cannot be a firm or group of people.

1.4 The Adjudicator takes the initiative in establishing facts and law,

and the adjudication is not expert determination,

Note that expert determination is a non-statutory process.

nor arbitration.

Note that arbitration is finally binding under the jurisdiction of the Arbitration Act 96.

The Adjudicator may rely on his own expert knowledge and experience.

1.5 The Decision is binding

until finally determined by arbitration or legal proceedings, or by agreement.

1.6 The parties must comply with the Decision without delay.

Payment is to be as contracted, in the next stage payment

unless directed otherwise under the payment provisions of The Act.

The Notice of Adjudication

2.1 Any party may at any time

give notice of intention to refer a dispute arising under the contract to adjudication by a written Notice of Adjudication to the other party, including

details and date of the contract,

issues to be decided,

details of the nature and extent of redress sought.

Appointment of the Adjudicator

3.1 Where an Adjudicator has been agreed

or named in the contract,

then the referrer, at the same time as giving the Notice of Adjudication,

sends it to the Adjudicator

and requests confirmation of willingness to act

within 4 days of the date of the Notice.

3.2 Where an Adjudicator has not been agreed,

nor named in the contract,

then the referrer, with the Notice of Adjudication,

includes one or more names of adjudicators who are willing to act,

for one to be selected by the other party

within 4 days of the date of the Notice.

3.3 If confirmation under 3.1,

or selection under 3.2 have not occurred,

or the Adjudicator does not accept or is unwilling,

then either party may within 3 further days

request the person or body named in the contract,

or, if none, request the ICE

to appoint an Adjudicator, using the form of application,

with a copy of the Notice, and the fee.

3.4 The Adjudicator is appointed on the Adjudicator's Agreement and Schedule,

and is entitled to be paid a reasonable fee and expenses,

and the parties sign the Agreement within 7 days of request.

3.5 If for any reason the Adjudicator is unable to act,

either party may require appointment of a replacement as in 3.3.

Referral

4.1 The Referrer, within 2 days of receipt of confirmation under 3.1, or notification of selection under 3.2,

or appointment under 3.3;

sends to the Adjudicator, and copies to the other party:-

a statement of case including:-

a copy of the Notice of Adjudication,

a copy of any adjudication provision in the contract,

the information upon which he relies, with supporting documents.

4.2 The date of Referral is the date the Adjudicator receives documents as 4.1.

The Adjudicator advises the parties of the date forthwith.

Conduct of the Adjudication

5.1 The Adjudicator decides within 28 days of referral,

or within 14 more days with the consent of the Referrer,

or a longer period agreed by the parties after referral.

5.2 The Adjudicator determines the matters set out in the Notice of Adjudication,

and any other matters which the parties and the Adjudicator agree to add.

5.3 The Adjudicator may open up, review, and revise:-

any decision (other than an adjudicator's, unless the parties agree),

or opinion, instruction, direction, certificate, or valuation made under or in connection with the contract and which is relevant.

The Adjudicator may order payment of money,

or other redress,

but no decision of the Adjudicator affects the freedom of the parties, the Engineer or other authorised person to vary the Works.

5.4 The other party may respond within 14 days of referral,

or longer period agreed between the parties and the Adjudicator.

5.5 The Adjudicator has complete discretion in how to conduct the adjudication,

and establishes the procedure and timetable,

subject to the contract and The Act.

He shall not be required to observe any rule of evidence.

He may:-

ask for further written information;

meet and question the parties and their representatives;

visit the site;

request the production of documents;

request the attendance of people whom he considers could assist;

set times for the above;

proceed to decide even if a party fails to provide information,

to attend a meeting,

or to take any other requested action;

issue further directions as he considers appropriate.

5.6 The Adjudicator may obtain legal or technical advice,

having notified the parties of his intention.

5.7 Any party may at any time

request that additional parties be joined in the Adjudication, subject to the agreement of the Adjudicator and the existing and additional parties.

Additional parties have the same rights and obligations as the other parties,

unless otherwise agreed by the Adjudicator and the parties.

The Decision

6.1 The Adjudicator decides within the time limit in 5.1,

and may decide different aspects at different times.

The Adjudicator shall not be required to give reasons.

Note that this does not prevent the Adjudicator giving reasons if he is willing to do so following a request.

6.2 The Adjudicator may direct payment of interest,

simple or compound,

at rates,

and between dates or events,

as he considers appropriate.

Note that he is not limited to interest provisions in the contract.

6.3 If the Adjudicator fails to reach and notify a decision within the time limit,

a party may give 7 days notice of intention to refer to a replacement.

6.4 If the Adjudicator fails to reach and notify a decision within the time limit,

but does so before referral to a replacement,

the decision is effective.

If the parties are not notified,

then the decision has no effect and the Adjudicator is not paid,

but legal or technical advisers under 5.6 are paid for advice received.

6.5 The parties bear their own costs and expenses.

The parties are jointly and severally liable for the Adjudicator's fees and expenses, including his advisers under 5.6,

and should pay in equal shares,

but the Adjudicator may allocate the shares differently.

6.6 Up to 7 days before the decision is due, the Adjudicator may give notice that he will deliver it only on full payment of his fees and expenses,

and any party who pays and obtains the decision may recover the other party's share as a debt due.

Note that payment before delivery is normal practice in arbitration also.

6.7 The parties are entitled to the relief and remedies set out,

and may seek summary enforcement regardless of litigation or arbitration.

Note that a court will only require evidence that the Adjudicator has written the decision in appropriate form, that actions as directed have not been given by the directed time, or, if none, a reasonable time. The court will not enquire whether the Adjudicator was right. It will order compliance as though the decision was a court order.

No issue previously decided by an adjudicator may be laid before another unless the parties agree.

6.8 The Adjudicator's decision does not inhibit a court or arbitrator in subsequent proceedings.

6.9 Clerical mistake, error, or ambiguity may be corrected within 7 days.

by the Adjudicator's initiative,

or party's request within 14 days of notification of the decision.

Miscellaneous Provisions

7.1 The Adjudicator may not become Arbitrator under the contract,

unless the parties agree.

The Adjudicator may not be called as a witness in proceedings on the subject of the adjudication.

7.2 The Adjudicator, his employee or agent is not liable for anything done or omitted, except in bad faith,

and the parties jointly and severally indemnify them against third party claims.

7.3 The ICE, its servants or agents are not liable for action, omission or misconduct.

7.4 All notices are to be sent recorded delivery to the address in the contract,

or, if none, to the principal place of business or registered office.

Any agreement under the adjudication procedure is to be in writing.

7.5 The procedure is to be in accordance with the law of the contract.

Definitions and reference to particular ICE agreements follow the Procedure in ICE documentation.

Appendix F — CIC Model Adjudication Procedure (MAP)

The Construction Industry Council, which represents professional institutions and trade bodies, made recommendations to Government on the drafting of both the Housing Grants, Construction, and Regeneration Act 1996 and The Scheme for Construction Contracts 1998 which were not all taken up. The CIC has made the Model Adjudication Procedure (MAP) which complies with The Act but which differs from The Scheme. It is intended to be available throughout the industry as an alternative to The Scheme and JCT Rules.

It is proposed that MAP will be applied by the professional institutions in their published standard forms of agreement for professional services. The Association of Consultant Architects uses MAP in its form of construction contract.

It must be borne in mind that unless specific rules are incorporated in the contract or agreement in accordance with The Act, The Scheme for Construction Contracts will apply by default.

The following is an outline of the provisions of MAP, with comments. For the full text see the Model which is available from CIC.

General Principles

1 The object of adjudication under this procedure is to reach a fair, rapid and inexpensive decision.

2 The Adjudicator shall act impartially.

The Adjudicator may take the initiative in ascertaining fact and law.

He may use his own knowledge and experience.

The adjudication is not arbitration nor expert determination.

CIC envisages that the adjudicator will be an expert and will understand the matters in dispute but statutory adjudication is a separate process from arbitration which is done under the more onerous provisions of the Arbitration Act 1996. Expert determination is a process in which the expert makes decisions about how work is to be carried out and may take on liabilities for design and specification in determining the work. The adjudicator will only decide matters in accordance with the contract; he will not change design or specifications.

4 The decision is binding until otherwise determined in arbitration or litigation.

This is as required by The Act.

5 The decision is to be immediately implemented by the parties.

Application

6 The current edition of MAP applies if incorporated in a contract.

7 MAP applies if in conflict with adjudication procedure in the contract.

Appointment of the Adjudicator

8 Notice of Adjudication is given by either party, the referring party to the other party,

including a brief statement of issues and redress sought,

and copied to the adjudicator if he is named in the contract.

Note that MAP does not refer to multi-party contracts in which the same principles would apply. The Scheme for Construction Contracts has more specific requirements which might be applied under MAP.

9 The object of 10 - 14 is to appoint and refer to the adjudicator within 7 days of the Notice of Adjudication.

10 The parties agree a name within 2 days of the Notice.

Alternatively:-

If an adjudicator is named in the contract:-
he confirms availability within 2 days of receiving the Notice.

Or If no adjudicator is named:-
or a named adjudicator does not confirm within 2 days,
then the referring party requests nomination within 5 days:-
if an adjudicator nominating body is named in the contract,
by that body,
or if none, by the CIC,
and attaches the Notice of Adjudication, and the fee.

11 If the adjudicator is unable to act,

or if he fails to decide within the timescale

either party may request a body, as in 10, to appoint a replacement.

12 The adjudicator is appointed on the MAP Agreement

and is entitled to reasonable fees and expenses.

Note that 12 appears to preclude any particular conditions which the adjudicator may wish to include as a term of his engagement such as secure payment in advance. It is likely that adjudicators will have their own terms and failure to accept them might result in the adjudicator's declining the appointment. See also below where 20 provides the power for the adjudicator to withhold the decision until he has been paid. 25 provides that he will not be paid for a late decision.

13 A party's objection to his appointment does not invalidate the appointment or any decision he might make.

Conduct of the Adjudication

14 Within 7 days of the Notice of Adjudication,

or if later, as soon as the adjudicator is appointed,

the referrer sends to the adjudicator, and copies to the other party:-

a statement of case,

a copy of the Notice,

the contract,

details of circumstances giving rise to the dispute,

reasons for redress sought,

evidence to be relied upon.

15 The date of referral is the date on which the Adjudicator receives the statement of case.

Note that MAP differs here from The Scheme for Construction Contracts which makes the date of the Referral Notice the effective date.

16 The adjudicator must decide within 28 days of the date of referral,

or a 14 days extension agreed by the referrer,

or a longer period agreed by the parties after referral.

17 The adjudicator has complete discretion over conduct,

and establishes procedure and timetable,

and is not required to observe any court or other rule of evidence or procedure.

In particular he may:-

i. request written defence or arguments,

ii. request production of documents, or people to attend,

iii. visit the site

iv. meet and question parties and their representatives,

v. meet parties separately,

vi. limit the time for submission of statements, defence or argument,

vii. proceed in the absence of compliance with a request or direction,

viii. issue further directions as appropriate.

These provisions give the adjudicator wide scope to ensure that he gets all of the information he may need and to proceed to a decision within the time allowed.

18 The parties must comply with the adjudicator's requests or directions.

19 The adjudicator may obtain legal or technical advice,

provided he notifies the parties of his intention,

and he must provide copies of any written advice obtained.

The implication of 19 is that the adjudicator may incur costs in obtaining advice which the parties will have to pay for. By notifying them of his intention he provides them with the opportunity to object, though he may still proceed and the party might then only object that the cost was unreasonably incurred.

20 The adjudicator must decide the matters set out in the notice of adjudication,

and any other matters agreed by him and the parties.

This limitation of tri-partite agreement differs from The Scheme which provides more complex procedure for additional matters.

21 The adjudicator applies the law of the contract in determining the parties' rights and obligations.

Although an expert versed in contract law, the adjudicator will not usually be a lawyer, and the parties may wish to present argument regarding the law for him to consider, and if necessary for him to obtain legal advice under 19.

22 Additional parties may be joined in the adjudication,

provided the adjudicator and the new and original parties agree, and the new parties have the same rights and obligations as the original parties,

unless the adjudicator and the parties agree otherwise.

This provision for additional parties to be joined means that where more than one party might be at fault, or have a claim, they can be included so that all are dealt with in the adjudicator's decision. However, since the adjudicator can only deal with matters under the contract, he will not be able to decide matters which extend outside the contract, such as sub-contracts or independent contracts. Such a situation might be dealt with under parallel adjudications so that the adjudicator can deal with a bunch of related matters. The timescale and the dates of referral might make such a procedure difficult to effect.

23 The adjudicator may resign at any time on giving written notice.

The Decision

24 The adjudicator shall decide within the time limits,

but he may withhold delivery until he has been paid,

The provision to give the adjudicator a lien over delivery of the decision comes from normal practice in arbitration. The adjudicator, having determined a dispute, perhaps involving a party who is reluctant to pay bills, or where neither party has achieved its objective and both are disappointed, does not want to have to chase the parties through the courts to get his own payments.

and he shall not be required to give reasons.

MAP, in providing that the adjudicator shall not be required to give reasons, differs from The Scheme where either party may request reasons. There is no reason why a party should not ask the adjudicator for reasons with the decision and the adjudicator may agree, provided that the other party does not object, and that he is paid for the time taken to present reasons.

25 If the adjudicator is late in reaching his decision, it will still be effective provided that it is reached before a replacement adjudicator is appointed under 11.

If he fails to reach an effective decision he is not entitled to payment except for legal or technical advice passed on to the parties.

26 The adjudicator may open up, review and revise any of the following made in relation to the contract:-

certificate,	decision,	direction,	instruction,
notice,	opinion,	requirement,	or valuation.

This clause gives the adjudicator very wide powers to intervene. The Scheme only includes decisions or certificates. Bearing in mind that the adjudicator will not have power to change the design or specification, he is unlikely to intervene without the express invitation of one of the parties and he will need to be convinced that such intervention is justified under the contract terms.

27 The adjudicator may direct payment of interest, simple or compound, from such dates, and at such rates, as he considers appropriate.

Where The Scheme limits the adjudicator to interest which arises under the terms of the contract, MAP appears to allow him to decide interest for other reasons, such as delay in payment during the period of the dispute. He will also be able to look into payment against the provisions of The Act s.109 - 113, and The Scheme Part II which may entitle a party to payment over the terms of the contract and this entitlement may lead him into awarding interest on overdue sums.

28 The parties shall bear their own costs and expenses incurred in the adjudication.

There are two categories of cost, those of the parties, covered by this clause, and those of the adjudicator, by 29. If a party obtains expert opinion to assist his case, that will be a party cost and must be paid by the party under 28.

If the adjudicator obtains expert opinion that cost will be part of his expenses and will be dealt with under 30.

29 For the adjudicator's fees and expenses including those of any legal or technical adviser appointed under 19:-

the parties are jointly and severally liable,

and they should pay equal shares,

but the adjudicator may direct a different allocation

or if the adjudication does not proceed to a decision,

the referrer will pay.

The provision for the adjudicator to allocate payment of his charges by a particular party means that he can follow the normal principles of costs in court or arbitration, where, broadly, the loser pays the winner's costs. In MAP he cannot allocate party costs.

The provision that the referrer pays the adjudication costs for an uncompleted adjudication means that he pays if he withdraws or if he reaches settlement with his adversary. He may wish to make these costs a matter of issue in settlement negotiations.

Enforcement

30 A party, being entitled to redress set out in a decision, may seek summary enforcement, whether or not the dispute is referred to final determination by arbitration or litigation.

No issue decided by an adjudicator may be referred to another adjudicator unless the parties agree to do so.

For summary enforcement the party will apply to a court and the judge will grant the application on the adjudicator's decision without considering the merits of the case. If a party then fails to provide redress, he will be in contempt of court and liable to fine or imprisonment.

He should first comply and then take the matter to arbitration or to court himself. This provision is weaker than the similar provision in The Scheme which relies on a peremptory order by the adjudicator for summary enforcement.

31 If, after adjudication, a dispute is taken to arbitration or to court, the court or the arbitrator may ignore the adjudication as though it had never occurred.

Further proceedings will not be in the nature of an appeal against the adjudication; they will amount to a fresh hearing. The value of the adjudication will be that it has provided a working decision in the interim before it may be found otherwise.

Miscellaneous Provisions

32 If the dispute goes on to arbitration, the adjudicator may not become the arbitrator of the same dispute unless the parties agree.

The adjudicator may not be called as a witness in subsequent proceedings.

33 Except in bad faith, neither the adjudicator, nor his employee or agent, shall be liable for his acts or omissions.

There is no provision for the correction of errors. If he makes a genuine mistake the adjudicator should take steps to correct it without delay whether it is found by a party or by himself. To fail to correct an error could amount to negligence and any delay might be construed to be in bad faith.

34 The adjudicator is appointed to determine a dispute between the parties and may not be relied upon by third parties to whom he owes no duty of care.

This provision arises because any decision of an adjudicator will be made under a pre-existing contract between the parties and any external effect of the decision will be an effect of the contract for which the parties are liable.

35 MAP applies in accordance with the law of England and Wales.

MAP is drafted for England and Wales. It should not be used in other jurisdictions.

Appendix G — CEDR Rules for Adjudication

In accordance with The Centre for Dispute Resolution's objective that the rules for Alternative Dispute Resolution (ADR) methods should be as few as possible in order for the tribunal to have as full discretion over the procedure as possible consistent with any over-riding rules, CEDR Rules for Adjudication are short and limited to facilitating a speedy decision under The Act. CEDR, being both a professional association and a commercial provider of dispute resolution services has published a draft adjudication clause for insertion in contracts, and a form of agreement for adjudicator's services through CEDR.

The following commentary summarises the provisions of the CEDR Rules, with notes. Reference to the full text should be made before relying on this commentary.

Model Adjudication Clause

CEDR publishes two alternative model clauses for inserting in contracts.

Alternative A, with Decision binding after 60 days

A long clause which introduces a provision to make the Decision of the Adjudicator binding by default if no Notice of Dissatisfaction is issued within 60 days of the date of the Decision.

Alternative B

A short clause:-

> "Any dispute arising under this Agreement which cannot be resolved amicably between the Parties shall, in the first instance, be referred to adjudication in accordance with the Rules for Adjudication of CEDR at present in force."

Note that this clause could be used in any agreement and CEDR or any other rules could be given.

Appointment of Adjudicator and reference to Adjudication

A If the parties are unable to agree on an Adjudicator, this procedure will apply:-

(i) Either Party may apply to CEDR to appoint an Adjudicator.

(ii) CEDR's application form, or an acceptable form is sent, containing:-

names and addresses of the parties,

copy of the contract adjudication provision,

brief details of the dispute,

other relevant information,

brief statement of redress sought,

(iii) with CEDR's appointment fee.

(iv) CEDR appoints an Adjudicator within 7 days,

copies the application to the Adjudicator,

sends the Adjudicator's details to the Parties.

B The Parties and the Adjudicator promptly agree using CEDR's form.

C Where the Adjudicator is named in the contract,

or the Parties agree a name,

the Referrer gives notice to the Adjudicator,

with details as A (ii),

and the Adjudicator confirms acceptance under CEDR Rules.

D The Date of Referral shall be:-

Where A applies, the date of the appointment by CEDR.

Where C applies, the date when the Parties are given the Adjudicator's confirmation.

E Parties who have agreed to submit to Adjudication under these rules are bound by them.

Rules of Conduct of the Adjudication Procedure

1 The Adjudicator is:-

free to take the initiative in ascertaining facts and law,

to have complete discretion as to how to conduct the Adjudication,

not required to observe rules of evidence or procedure of court etc.,

to have discretion whether to hold any meeting with the Parties,

not to consider any statement which the Parties do not have available.

2 Within 2 days of Referral the adjudicator either

establishes a procedure other than below,

or fixes a preliminary meeting within 7 days of Referral.

3 Within 4 days of Referral the referrer submits

a concise statement of the issues and facts, with copy documents

and within 7 days of receipt, the other parties submit

a concise statement of response, with copy documents.

4 At any time the Adjudicator may request

information, documents, access to property

and the Parties will respond promptly.

5 The Adjudicator may obtain legal or specialist advice

subject to informing the Parties,

and to their consent.

6 If a Party fails to comply with requests,

the Adjudicator may proceed regardless.

7 The Adjudicator shall decide the referred matters,

impartially and in good faith,

and shall have power to review and revise under the contract

any decision to which the dispute relates.

8 The Adjudicator may vary the periods specified,

except for the time for decision.

Decision of the Adjudicator

9 The Adjudicator shall:-

decide as soon as practicable,

with the object of deciding within 14 days of Referral,

may, but is not obliged to, give reasons for the Decision,

in any event decide within 28 days of Referral.

The time may be extended:-

up to 14 days with the Referrer's consent,

or any period agreed by the Parties,

but if the Adjudicator requests extension and the Parties refuse,

the Adjudicator shall decide within the time, as appropriate.

10 The Parties are jointly and severally liable for fees, expenses

and adviser's charges under 5.

The Adjudicator is entitled to withhold the decision pending payment.

The Adjudicator has discretion to apportion liability between the Parties.

Notice of Dissatisfaction

12 Within 60 days of notice of the Decision, or longer if agreed,

a Party may give Notice of Dissatisfaction

to the other Party and the Adjudicator,

failing which the Decision is final and binding.

Note that this provision is not found in most other adjudication rules. It is in the ICE procedure.

13 If Notice of Dissatisfaction is given,

the dispute is to be determined in arbitration or in court as contracted,

and the tribunal is not bound by the decision, and can review it.

Incapacity of the Adjudicator

14 If the Adjudicator becomes unable or unwilling to act, he gives notice, and the Parties appoint a replacement within 7 days,

or CEDR appoints one within 7 days of an application.

Mediation Option

15 At any time before the Decision,

the Parties may agree to refer to mediation,

and notify the Adjudicator to suspend the Adjudication,

the mediation being non-binding until settlement is agreed in writing.

The Adjudicator may not be the mediator.

The Parties agree on a Mediator within 7 days,

or CEDR appoints one.

If settlement is not made within 28 days the Adjudication resumes.

Liability of the Adjudicator and CEDR

16 Neither CEDR nor the Adjudicator, nor their employees or agents,

is liable for anything done or omitted,

except in bad faith.

Notices

17 A copy of every notice or document sent to CEDR or the Adjudicator or issued by the Adjudicator

shall be sent at the same time to the Parties

and treated as delivered within 2 days by post,

or the same day by fax or hand delivery during normal office hours.

Appendix H — ORSA Adjudication Rules

The Official Referees' (OR) courts are in a division of the High Court which specialises in construction cases. The Official Referees Solicitors Association (ORSA) represents solicitors who practice in the OR courts and in construction arbitration. ORSA has produced rules for adjudication and is an Adjudicator Nominating Body.

The following commentary summarises the provisions of the ORSA Adjudication Rules - 1998 Version 1.2, with notes. Reference to the full text should be made before relying on this commentary.

Adjudication Clause

ORSA Rules are intended for inclusion in contracts with a clause on the following lines:-

"Any dispute arising under this agreement shall in the first instance be referred to adjudication in accordance with the ORSA Adjudication Rules."

The rules may also be used by agreement between the parties where such a clause is not used. They should not be adapted for an adjudication which is not under ORSA nomination or to be subject to ORSA administration.

ORSA also recommends that if a contract contains an arbitration clause, then in order to prevent enforcement difficulties arising out of S.9 of The Arbitration Act 1996, (Stay of Legal Proceedings), the arbitration clause should contain wording along the following lines:-

"...provided always that the enforcement of any decision of an adjudicator is not a matter which may be referred to arbitration."

The rules provide wide discretion for the adjudicator to get on with determining the dispute but also retain a degree of control for ORSA to re-establish control in case things go wrong.

Procedural Rules

1 (i) ORSA Adjudication Rules incorporated in a contract will be the most recent edition at the time of the notice of adjudication.

(ii) The Rules meet The Act and The Scheme does not apply.

2 Definitions are given.

Commencement

3 (i) The Rules apply upon any party giving written notice requiring adjudication and identifying the dispute.

Note that ORSA refers throughout to the "notice requiring adjudication."

(ii) Within 7 days of the notice, the adjudicator under Rule 6, 7(ii), or 8 gives written notice of acceptance.

(iii) The date of the referral is the date the adjudicator confirms acceptance.

Note that ORSA's referral date is different from other rules which use the date of the notice, or the date of receipt.

4 Notice requiring adjudication may be given at any time whether or not litigation or arbitration has started.

5 More notices may be given under a contract.

Appointment

6 A person who is agreed by the parties and confirms acceptance within 7 days of the notice is the adjudicator.

7 Where no adjudicator has been agreed or confirmed acceptance, a party applies to ORSA for nomination:-

(i) application in writing, with:-

copy of the contract or evidence of agreement to ORSA Rules,

and of the written notice

and ORSA's appointment fee (£100).

(ii) Chairman of ORSA endeavours to secure appointment within 7 days of the notice.

(iii) A person so appointed, ready and willing, is the adjudicator.

8 ORSA Chairman may give notice and replace the adjudicator after complaint from a party, and the previous adjudicator's directions and decisions remain in force until reviewed and replaced by the new adjudicator's. Timescales restart from the date of replacement.

9 An adjudicator for a dispute may be appointed for another dispute arising in the contract.

10 An agreement to the rules by a party is an offer to ORSA, and to the adjudicator, to abide by the rules, accepted by appointing an adjudicator or starting the adjudication.

Note that this effectively makes a contract between the parties with ORSA and the adjudicator.

Scope of the Adjudication

11 The scope is the matters identified in the notice requiring adjudication and

(i) any further matters as agreed by the parties,

(ii) any further matters which the adjudicator determines must be included for the adjudication to be effective and meaningful.

12 The adjudicator may rule on his own jurisdiction and the scope.

Purpose of Adjudication & Role of the Adjudicator

13 The purpose is to resolve disputes rapidly and economically.

14 The adjudicator's decision shall be binding until determined otherwise by arbitration (if in the contract) or legal proceedings.

15 Where possible, the decision shall represent the legal entitlements of the parties, or, where it cannot, the fair and reasonable view of the adjudicator in the light of facts and law which have been ascertained.

16 The adjudicator has the same power to open up and review certificates and other things as an arbitrator and/or the courts.

17 The adjudicator acts fairly and impartially but not as an arbitrator.

Conduct of the Adjudication

18 The adjudicator establishes procedure and timetable.

19 He may if he thinks fit:-

(i) Require delivery of written statements of case;

(ii) Require a party to produce a bundle of key documents, and draw inference from a failure to produce them;

(iii) Require documents that would be privileged at court;

(iv) Limit length of written and oral submissions;

(v) Require attendance for questioning of a party, a party's employee or agent;

(vi) Make site visits;

(vii) Make use of his specialist knowledge;

(viii) Provided one party requests or consents, obtain specialist's advice;

(ix) Meet or communicate with a party alone;

(x) Make oral or written directions for conduct;

(xi) Review and revise his own directions;

(xii) Conduct the adjudication by questioning;

and take initiative in ascertaining facts and law;

(xiii) Reach a decision with or without a meeting, or endeavouring to facilitate settlement.

Note the implication here that the adjudicator might facilitate settlement. This is weaker but has a similar effect to the mediation clause in CEDR's Rules although CEDR's adjudicator will not mediate.

20 The adjudicator shall exercise powers fairly and impartially, giving the parties reasonable opportunity of putting their cases and dealing with their opponent's.

21 The adjudicator may not:-

(i) Require any advance payment or security for fees,

Note that other rules permit advanced payment or a lien on the decision in line with normal practice in arbitration.

(ii) Receive written submissions which are not available to the other side,

(iii) Refuse the right of a party to be represented at a hearing,

iv) Act in the face of a conflict of interest,

(v) Require a party to contribute to the legal costs of another party.

22 The adjudicator shall decide within 28 days of referral,

or a longer period agreed by the parties after referral,

or he may extend by up to 14 days with the referrer's consent.

Adjudicator's Fees and Expenses

23 A party who requests adjudication without entitlement is solely responsible for the adjudicator's fees and expenses.

24 Otherwise, the parties are jointly and severally liable for the adjudicator's fees and expenses , including his advisers', in equal shares unless directed otherwise.

25 The adjudicator's fees shall not exceed £1000 per day or part day plus expenses and VAT.

Note that these are the only rules which I have seen which enter the realms of payment; most allow reasonable charges to be made.

Decisions

26 The adjudicator may direct payment of compound or simple interest as commercially reasonable.

27 Decisions shall be in writing,

but shall not include reasons.

Enforcement

28 Every decision shall be implemented without delay,

the parties being entitled to reliefs and remedies as set out,

and to summary enforcement regardless of any challenge or review,

and there shall be no set-off, counterclaim, or abatement in enforcement proceedings.

Immunity, Confidentiality and non-Compellability

29 Neither ORSA , its Chairman or deputy,

nor the Adjudicator,

nor employee or agent of them,

shall be liable for anything done or not done,

in negligence or otherwise,

unless in bad faith.

30 The adjudication and all matters are to be kept confidential,

except as necessary for implementation, enforcement, or further proceedings.

31 In any subsequent arbitration or legal proceedings,

the adjudicator shall not be:-

joined as a party,

subpoenaed,

required to give evidence or to provide his notes.

Law

32 The rules are governed by English law under English Courts.

33 Except in the case of the adjudicator's bad faith,

no party shall apply to court in relation to the conduct or a decision in the adjudication,

until the adjudicator has decided, or refused to decide,

and until the party has complied with any decision.

Appendix I — Bibliography

Statutory Instruments

The Housing Grants, Construction and Regeneration Act 1996,
SI 1998 No. 650, HMSO.

The Scheme for Construction Contracts (England and Wales) Regulations 1998,
SI 1998 No. 649, HMSO.

The Scheme for Construction Contracts (Scotland) Regulations 1998,
SI 1998 No. 687 (S.34), HMSO.

The Construction Contracts (England and Wales) Exclusion Order 1998,
SI 1998 No. 648, HMSO.

Non-Government Adjudication Rules and Procedures

Joint Contracts Tribunal (JCT) Standard Form of Building Contract, 1980 Edition, Amendment 18, and similar amendments effective 1 May 98 to other JCT Standard Forms,
RIBA Publications, Finsbury Mission, 39 Moreland St., London, EC1V 8BB.

Construction Industry Council (CIC) Model Adjudication Procedure (MAP), 1st Edition, Feb. 98,
CIC, 26 Store St., London, WC1E 7BT.

Institution of Civil Engineers (ICE) Adjudication Procedure, (1997) published 1998,
Thomas Telford Publishing, Thomas Telford Services Ltd., 1 Heron Quay, London, E14 4JD.

Centre for Dispute Resolution (CEDR) Rules for Adjudication, 1st Edition , May 98,
CEDR, Princes House, 95 Gresham Street, London, EC2V 7NA.

Official Referees Solicitors Association (ORSA) Adjudication Rules - 1998, Version 1.2,
ORSA c/o Nicholson Graham & Jones, 110 Cannon St., London, EC4N 6AR.

Other Publications Available or in Preparation

Campbell, P. et al (1997) *Construction Disputes,* Whittles Publishing.

CIC, (1998) *The Guide to Construction Adjudication*, London, Construction Industry Council, as CICMAP above.

Cottam, G. (1998) *Adjudication under the Scheme for Construction Contracts,* Thomas Telford Publishing, as ICE above.

Timpson, J & Totterdill, B. (1998) *Adjudication for Architects and Engineers,* Thomas Telford Publishing.

Totterdill, B. (1998) *ICE Adjudication Procedure:- A User's Guide and Commentary,* Thomas Telford Publishing.